Moments *of the* HEART

Endorsements for
Moments *of the* HEART

"The book is very powerful and beautiful. It is passionate, spiritual, and well-reasoned—three things that don't always go together. I love the analysis of the word *matzpun* and its variety of related meanings. I was profoundly moved by the journey Horenstein took."

–**Rabbi Joseph Telushkin**, author of *A Code of Jewish Ethics*

"I highly recommend this book for anyone seeking guidance and direction for improving one's life by drawing on the wisdom found in the texts of Judaism. This is a thoughtful and insightful work of an Israeli-American woman which speaks directly from the heart."

–**Rabbi Joshua Stampfer**, Rabbi Emeritus
of Congregation Neveh Shalom

"Veteran educator Dorice Horenstein brings her passion for learning and healing to each page of *Moments of the Heart*. Everyone will find something new in the connections she creates between Hebrew language, Jewish concepts, and Jewish spirituality."

–**Mel Berwin**, Director of Congregational
Learning of Congregation Neveh Shalom

"As Dorice beautifully explains in the beginning of this book, the heart is at the core of everything we do. Yet, today's world moves fast. We react rather than respond. We forget to take a moment and check in with ourselves. *Moments of the Heart* brings us back to center, to what is important in life. The discussions, lessons, and practices shared in this book reconnect us to the core of ourselves and of our community. This book returns us to our heart and is especially relevant to those in leadership who are working, sometimes at great odds, to build a more compassionate and healthier world."

–**Lisa Berkley**, Ph.D., Councilwoman in Marina, CA

"Dorice has written a book with heart that combines her own modern take on life with that of ancient Jewish wisdom. If you are at a turning point in your life, this precious book most likely will speak to you."

—**Cherie Koller Fox**, Jewish Chaplaincy Council of Massachusetts and the Rabbi Emerita at Congregation Eitz Chayim in Cambridge, MA

Moments *of* *the* HEART

Four Relationships Everyone Should Have to Live WHOLEheartedly

Dorice Horenstein

NEW YORK

LONDON • NASHVILLE • MELBOURNE • VANCOUVER

Moments *of the* HEART
Four Relationships Everyone Should Have to Live WHOLEheartedly

© 2020 Dorice Horenstein

Published in New York, New York, by Morgan James Publishing. Morgan James is a trademark of Morgan James, LLC. www.MorganJamesPublishing.com

ISBN 978-1-64279-403-8 paperback
ISBN 978-1-64279-404-5 eBook
Library of Congress Control Number: 2018914472

Cover Design by:
Rachel Lopez
www.r2cdesign.com

Editor:
Jennifer McGrath

In an effort to support local communities, raise awareness and funds, Morgan James Publishing donates a percentage of all book sales for the life of each book to Habitat for Humanity Peninsula and Greater Williamsburg.

Get involved today! Visit
www.MorganJamesBuilds.com

These moments are what make life worth living.
To my loving family from near and far,
with blessings for health,
both of body and spirit.

Contents

Foreword

When Dorice Horenstein first showed me a copy of her book, I had no idea what to expect. I was pleased to discover that *Moments of the Heart* was a guide book, not to Israel or any other country for that matter, but a guide book to better living, based on Jewish values and insights.

This book draws upon an extensive knowledge of the Bible and an intimate acquaintance with the Hebrew language. What particularly attracts me is that *Moments of the Heart* deals with the universal human problems we all face in the course of life. Every person encounters problems, resulting in the need to make decisions that can affect the future.

So what do we do? We seek guidance and direction to make the best possible decision. Whether mending personal relationships, confronting medical crises, or dealing with legal complications, we consult with experts in various fields, read books and articles, or explore every source of information that we can find to ensure the best decision.

Moments of the Heart made me think of Rabbi Kushner's book *When Bad Things Happen to Good People*, which has such a powerful impact upon all people who search for guidance in the great problems they face.

Ms. Horenstein opens up a wide door to the world of Jewish thought and experiences accumulated over many hundreds of years of life under all kinds of situations. She does this in a warm and understanding manner, sensitive to our needs and our desires. She encourages our search for peace and truth. She weaves together the courage of Israel, the spirit of America, and, most important of all, the eternal soul of Judaism in our quest for the good life.

–**Rabbi Joshua Stampfer**, Rabbi Emeritus of
Congregation Neveh Shalom, Portland, OR

Author's Note

My Personal Lev Moment

In October 2014, my youngest sister was diagnosed with breast cancer. She was thirty-eight years old and living in Israel. Since I was living in the United States, I could not get up and drive to visit her. I could not hug her or share time together just sitting next to each other, so I had no other choice but to come up with something I could do 10,000 miles away to not only keep in touch, but also to remain positive along the way.

It was a Friday night when I received the news. I recall that day very clearly. My synagogue holds Friday night *Kabbalat Shabbat* (greeting the Sabbath) services and a lovely traditional dinner. Usually, I would look forward to going, but not that particular weekend. I had sadness in my heart and heaviness on my chest; I needed to stay by myself. I urged my husband to go with our son, and I was left in our quiet home all alone.

For the three hours they were gone, I did not leave my place on the sofa. I did not turn on the TV; I did not look at the news or watch any of my favorite shows. I did not read either. I just stared at the kitchen cabinets in front of me, focused on nothing and lost in my thoughts.

It is amazing what can happen when you empty your mind. New ideas enter. The seed for this book was born.

When my family returned and my husband walked through the door, he saw a resolution in my face. He would tell you that he saw a glimmer of excitement. I say that there was hope! I had made plans to launch a Facebook page called *Lev Moments*, where I would share once each week an uplifting message for the coming week. I combined the Hebrew word *lev*, which means "heart," with the English word *moments*. I later used these words to create the title of this book *Moments of the Heart*. I designed a logo with my good friend Lisa Berkley, and we were ready to go! The day was chosen. Saturday night was my first night. As we bid farewell to *Shabbat*, as many traditional Jews do on Saturday night when three stars are seen in the sky, my youngest son recorded as I spoke to the world words intended most for my sister. Then, we uploaded the video—that simple.

I began to feel better. I began to feel connected to my sister who was so far away. The two of us conversed about the *Lev Moments*, and I even surprised her four months later on her birthday by arriving in Israel and accompanying her to her weekly chemotherapy appointment.

I created these weekly videos for an entire year. During that year, I saw my sister go through hardships no one should ever have to experience. I saw her lose her hair and gain weight from the chemotherapy. But I also saw unexpected positive changes. She regained her inner strength and grew into her new self. I saw her husband and her children striving to be strong for her. I saw my mother and sisters pleading to God with questions unanswered. Why her? And all the while, I was recording and taping positive messages and putting them out to the universe. I initially started this project to benefit my sister, but I received much more in return.

These moments of the heart benefited me, and they benefited the people around me—those I worked with and those I lived with, those I liked and those I liked less, those I knew and those I didn't. Creating the weekly *Lev Moments* made me a better person. I used Hebrew, the magnificent God-made language, to illustrate different points and new ways to look at commonly used words. I learned a great deal as I created this deep library of material and wisdom— wisdom from our Jewish ancestors, making our life relevant and meaningful today more than ever.

At the end of a year, in the winter of 2015, I had recorded over fifty episodes, and I thought "What now?"

Now it is time for this book to be born. In the last year, I have composed, arranged, rewritten, and polished what has become the treasure you now hold in your hands. I have separated the book into four chambers, each one giving us a glimpse of different aspects of our relationships.

So sit back and take the first page into your hand. Don't rush through it. Do one entry a week, or however you feel led. Explore "Your Personal Lev Moments" with your children, with your partner, with your parents, with your colleagues, or with your boss. Create a book club for the year; offer the guidance within this book to a class of B'nai Mitzvah students. The possibilities are endless.

Each one of us brings to this life wisdom that is waiting to be discovered within ourselves. Discover yours and share your wisdom with others. Write in the spaces within this book wherever you see fit and let your answers be your guiding principles.

"לב טהור ברא–לי אלוהים ורוח נכון חדש בקרבי."—"Create for me a pure heart, O God, and renew a steadfast spirit within me" (Psalms 51:12). This verse highlights how, at times, we need guidance, help, and inspiration from a higher source. I know I needed that so I could not only create the videos in 2014 but bring this book to fruition now.

I have learned through the process of writing this book that what we hold inside our hearts—our thoughts, our feelings, our attitude—shapes us. If we become a manifestation of our hearts, let's take heed. By writing this book, I was given the gift of a fuller and more grateful heart. The process was not easy. At times, I had to dig deep and hold on to a lifeline to keep my head in line with my heart and my mind focused on being the best I can be. May it be for you, too, a reminder of who you want to be always. May this book open your mind to the right thoughts to put in your heart and the right actions to be manifested by your being.

My hope is that this book will help you become the best version of yourself possible.

"If you don't know what you're living for, you haven't yet lived."[1]
–Rabbi Noah Weinberg

A NOTE FROM MY SISTER

Part 1

A Facebook post from when she began her two-years-long battle with cancer.

"So… Today I began the journey of my life. Some of you know, and for those who don't… I have breast cancer. Yes… This disease… it does not know who it chose to mess with (and it's clear to you, my reader, that it will regret it). Today was my first chemotherapy session out of 16… The war on my life has begun.

Last night I initiated my bolding ritual… For those who don't know this ritual, it is the shaving of my head… It was very emotional. My brother and all my sisters… yes, all of them (through Skype my sister Dorice from America was able to join) were with me. And my two older nephews and a couple of dear friends were there as well. That was very empowering and demonstrated to me the amount of support

I have. So thank you all: to my extended family who is always interested and always willing to help, to my community, and neighbors. Here we go! To victory! To life! The fight for my life is beginning!

Bruria's message on Facebook to mark the shaving of her head and the beginning of treatment.

Gratitude

This book is the work of many. Without each and every one of these people, this book would not be in your hands today. I would like to mention all of you by your name and contribution.

First, I thank my youngest son, Yaniv, who recorded my original *Lev Moments* videos diligently for an entire year at the age of eleven in 2014. Not every child would assist his mother every Saturday night, but he did. He recorded the videos using a cell phone and then uploaded them to Facebook. I am so grateful. My heart and endless love go to you, Son.

To my daughter Hadas, who patiently read and provided wisdom and brilliant suggestions for every single word, concept, and theme— you provided guidance and priceless wisdom that I will forever treasure in my heart. I love you.

To my husband, Bob, and my son Matan for reading the manuscript more than once and providing insightful observations and grammatical changes as well as patiently looking up sources—I am forever thankful. I love you both.

My heartfelt and sincere gratitude and thanks are also due to my editor, Jennifer McGrath, for her patience in leading me through the process of how to put together a book worth reading, for her keen eye and attention to every single detail, word choice, and extra space throughout this book. You have taught me much. I am blessed our paths crossed, and I cannot thank you enough.

To my dear friend Lisa Berkley, thank you for believing in me when I was unable to envision what could be. Thank you for helping me design my Facebook page which one day became this book.

To my brother-in-law Michael Horenstein, of EZWriter Documentation Services, whose detailed proofreading of the completed manuscript was nothing shy of genius. Thank you so very much!

To Rabbi Stampfer, I extend to you a special heart-felt thank you for our bi-weekly meetings, for advising me along the way, for providing resources so that this book could see the light of day, and for being my constant inspiration of what a rabbi is. I am humbled to call you my rabbi.

To Cantor Ida Rae Cahana, Mel Berwin, Allison Fowler, Dale Foster, Sharon Erez, Shirona Lurie, Barbara Slader, and Rabbi Joseph Telushkin for taking time out of your precious and busy schedule to read part or all of my work and encouraging me to keep on going— you all provided insightful suggestions that helped make this book as strong as it is. I am deeply grateful.

To Yael Dassa for spending valuable hours combing through all the Hebrew and the transliteration to make sure all were correctly written and doing so with proficiency and willingness—I thank you and I cherish your kindness!

To Keith Berne who sat by me to help find citation and bibliography information for different *midrashim*—thank you for being a dedicated friend.

To Rabbi Motti Wilhelm, Chabad Lubavitch of Oregon, who verified citations for different Talmudic sources—thank you so much for your dedication and time!

And my daily gratitude and thanks to God who works this universe with wonder.

"ברוך אתה ה' אלוהינו מלך העולם

שהחיינו וקיימנו והגיענו לזמן הזה."

"Baruch atah Adonai Eloheinu, melech haolam,
she'hecheyanu, v'ki-y'manu, v'higi-anu lazman ha-zeh."
"Blessed are You, *HaShem* our God, King of the
universe, who has kept us alive, sustained us,
and brought us to this season"
(*The Complete Artscroll Siddur*, pp. 230–231).

Knock! Knock!

Who is it? Hello, this is Dorice. Dorice Horenstein. Thank you for inviting me in. I know I am not your friend yet, but I want you to know me. This will make your reading of this book so much more enjoyable and meaningful. Let's prepare a cup of tea, and let me share who I am and why I am writing this book, my first book.

I came to America from Israel at the age of twenty-one. I grew up in a wonderful family, with four other siblings and two terrific parents. We were not financially wealthy. I remember my mom worked three jobs at times just to keep the family afloat while my dad built homes as a contractor. I remember wearing hand-me-down clothes (which, by the way, I love doing with my girlfriends nowadays). I shared one room with my three sisters growing up, and I fondly recall talking late into the night, sharing secrets and crushes on boys as well as heart-wrenching love stories that went as quickly as they came. This sisterly intimacy affected how bonded we became, and there is not a week that goes by now without a phone call to my siblings or my parents.

I have always loved and felt proud of my homeland. At the age of eighteen, I enrolled in the army service. I was serving in the Israeli army when I met my husband. It was not love at first sight, but at second sight, as we often joke. Looking back at that time period, I can wholeheartedly say that my role in the army solidified who the young girl from a small town in central Israel would become. Through my service, I began to understand the complex fabric of the different personalities around me. I learned what makes a leader and what causes a leader to stay a leader. I experienced the great feelings of teamwork and togetherness, and I also saw the results and consequences of being alone and rejected from the group. Today I am the product of the experiences of that young soldier from decades ago.

Shortly after I arrived in America, with only a suitcase and $600 to my name (and with no coat in the middle of December in Portland, Oregon), it was obvious to me that I would need to do something related to my background. I earned my bachelor's degree in English literature because I love languages (as you will see shortly) and a certification to teach English as a second language. Despite this, I actually began my professional career by teaching Hebrew and all aspects of Judaism to both children and adults.

One of the accomplishments I am most proud of is that I have three wonderful children and a supportive spouse. My husband and I raised our children (who are now more adults than children) to become independent, healthy, and contributing members of the communities in which they all live.

For the last sixteen years, I worked as an education director at a synagogue. This experience provided me with fertile ground to explore issues of ethics and morality with blossoming teenagers prior to their Bar/Bat Mitzvahs as well as with their parents and other adults. I

have taught classes and led group discussions about various works
by Rabbi Joseph Telushkin, Rabbi Harold Kushner, Rabbi Jonathan
Sacks, and others. I was fortunate to help families with their existential
life questions, daily struggles, and successes! I took situations that
happened to me, my children, students, parents, and other congregants
and viewed them through the lens of Judaism—what would our rabbis
say? Rabbi Akiva, Maimonides, Rashi, Nachmanides, Rabbi Gamaliel,
as well as Rebbetzin Esther Jungreis, Nechama Leibowitz, Rabbi
Netter, Rabbi Joshua Stampfer and so many others were the teachers in
my classes and at the *Shabbat* table with my children and my husband,
a table we often shared with dear family and friends.

Living in America, I also have been privileged to learn from
forward thinkers such as Oprah Winfrey, Gabrielle Bernstein, Brené
Brown, and so many other spiritual teachers and mentors. I treasure
the feeling that I stand on shoulders of giants—Jews, as well non-Jews.
All of these individuals contributed to who Dorice Horenstein is.

And with that, I come to you with a new suitcase this time—
this one full of advice from what I have learned by watching, doing,
reading, and hearing. My suitcase full of experiences is now my gift to
you. Let's open it!

Explanation of the Four Chambers

This book is about the heart: our collective hearts and our individual heart. Rabbi Hillel Hazaken said, "To the place that my heart takes me, that is where my legs lead me" (Talmud *Bavili, Sukkah*, 53a). Our heart has a tremendous influence on how we view life, how we act, and how we build relationships. In the Bible, the word *heart*—or in Hebrew, *lev* (לב)— is mentioned no fewer than 202 times. We read in the Book of Psalms, "Test me, LORD, and try me, examine my heart and my mind" (26:2). Moreover, it says in Proverbs 4:23, "From every interdict, guard your heart for the issues of life [come] out of it."

Our heart is crucial to our existence. To stay sharp we need our brain, but without the heart pumping the blood, our brain may not function.

During biblical times, our heart was considered the seat of the intellect, and, through time and history, the heart has gained another dimension—the seat of emotions. The receiving of the Torah on Mount Sinai was a monumental event in history that forever changed the human relationship with God. Imagine Moses's anticipation of the changes to come for the Jewish people. Up to this point in the Bible, we based our relationship with God through our ancestors' connection to God. At the moment of receiving the Torah at Mount Sinai, we stand and declare: "WE will do, and WE will listen" or *"Na'aseh v'nishma"* (Exodus 24:7). We took the responsibility upon ourselves to be partners with God—partners in making this world a better place. This moment of establishing a deeper relationship with God is so monumental in the Bible that we now celebrate this event through the holiday of Shavuot, known in the non-Jewish world as the holiday of Pentecost. To be full partners with God, we need to engage our hearts.

The last letter in the Torah is *"lamed"* in the word *Yisrael* (Israel). The first letter in the Torah is *"bet"* in the word *beresheet*, meaning "in the beginning." If you put these two letters together, the word *lev* is formed. How beautiful to think that the entirety of the Torah—the stories, the morals, and the miracles—all fit inside the collective heart of the Jewish people!

As I was thinking about the development of our relationship with God in the Torah, the central prayer in Judaism, the *V'ahavta*, came to mind: "You shall love your God with all your heart and with all your soul and with all your might" (Deuteronomy 6:4). There is so much symbolism in the heart, the life-sustaining force of all bodies.

The human heart has four chambers, which to me represent four different types of relationships we experience—hence the four chambers in this book!

The first chamber represents our relationship with ourselves. How do we view ourselves and how do we become the best humans we are capable of being? I selected this chamber as the first for this book because the relationship we have with our own self is the foundational block for all that follows. If we do not love ourselves (I do not mean in a narcissistic way, but in the deep sense of internal appreciation), can we expect others to love us? This chamber serves as a self-check of your character. It is about acknowledging who you are and making the effort to act, feel, and be your best. Do you know you are a champion, a one-of-a-kind human? Do you have an appreciation of the person you are today? This chamber will provide you with tools to live a life of content that only you can.

The second chamber represents our relationship to other people: It is about our relationships with friends, colleagues, children, spouse, partner, family, and even strangers. How do we bring out the best in ourselves when relating to others? How do we bring out the best in them? How do we create a healthy and sustainable relationship? How do we overcome being too judgmental? How do you truly love others?

The third chamber represents our relationship to God. Some of us call this higher power simply "God," while others use names such as "The Creator" or "Nature" or "The Source of all Beings." Without getting into the religiosity of the matter or each person's level of observance, how do we perceive our being in relationship to something bigger than us? Do we remain true to ourselves at all times and represent our values as human beings operating under a higher sovereignty, even when doing so might be challenging? This chamber is about love, commitment, and seeking guidance from a higher power. It is about the concept of faith. How would you define faith within the context of your life?

I view faith as believing in something without proof, without being able to see it. A "leap of faith" is exactly that—leaping into the unknown. When we go to bed at night, we have faith that the night will end and morning will arrive as it has every other day. When we say "See you at five," we make an assumption that we will arrive at the desired location at five o'clock. There are many things in life we believe in, even without proof. The third chamber is all about feeling that faith and trusting that some things are not meant to be seen but, nonetheless, they still exist. For me, that faith is a belief in God.

As a Jewish person, I have chosen the fourth chamber to represent those events in our life that define us, such as the birth of our children, a marriage, a Bar Mitzvah, and even graduation. In addition, I also include here our relationship as Jews to Jewish life events, Israel, and being part of the Jewish people. How do these events cultivate our actions moving forward and how do they define us? How do we cultivate a love and connection to the "Jewish tribe"? How do we continue to foster a connection with Israel in modern times when anti-Semitism and criticism of the Jewish homeland is prevalent in many corners of the world?

Within each of the four chambers of this book, you will find several entries. You have read how I transformed my uplifting videos, created for my sister (and, really, for everyone), into many of the entries within these pages. The topic of each entry is relevant to the specific chambers that form *Moments of the Heart*.

I first introduce the topic as it relates to Jewish thought and practice. I utilize my Hebrew knowledge to dig deep and explore the concept further. Sometimes I use a word play and explain the root of a Hebrew word. At the end of each entry, I offer a *Lev Moment* opportunity where I give you tools (in the form of questions and suggested actions) to further explore your own experiences and thoughts. This is your opportunity to reflect on the entry in a deep and meaningful way to you and journal your responses if you feel this would benefit you. In this section you will also have the opportunity to practice new actions. Learning by doing has proven itself useful endless times. These *Lev Moments* are an invitation for spiritual growth. Exploring the *Lev Moments* in a pace that is suitable to you may benefit you in seeing and witnessing your spiritual growth.

Below are questions to consider relating to each of the four chambers.

Chamber One—Relationship to Self

How do we take care of ourselves? How do we guard our spirit so we remain kind and grateful? What are some of the ways you love yourself? For me, it is about the small act of giving or of some kindness I can do for others that makes me feel good about myself and therefore causes me to like myself more.

Chamber Two—Relationships with Others

How do you cultivate these relationships? In the age of cell phones, internet, texting, Facebook posting, may I dare suggest the small act of picking up the telephone and calling a person to see how they are doing? I think our society is bombarded with so much amazing technology that we may, at times, forget to reach out on a human level and talk voice-to-voice with another person or meet for a coffee face-to-face.

Chamber Three—Relationship with God

Do you believe there is a source of energy/influence/goodness that is beyond human interaction? Do you have a name for it? Is it Creator? Or is it God? What is your relationship with this entity? Do you pray? Do you feel that God listens to you? Do you feel that there is a power beyond the us and the now? Why do you feel the way you feel?

Chamber Four—Relationship with
Israel and Jewish Life Events

Have you visited Israel? How do you cultivate the relationship you have with Israel? How does it feel when you hear of anti-Semitic behaviors or actions? Are you proud of your Judaism? How do you show this? What are the events in your life you believe define who you are today? Was it the birth of your children? Your wedding? Your graduation? Have you attended a *Brit Milah*? Bar or Bat Mitzvah? Graduation ceremony? Wedding? Funeral? What wisdom can you share from your life experiences with those who are in the crossroads of these important junctions?

Dorice surprising her sister for her thirty-ninth birthday in Israel in February of 2015.

I hope this book will be a source of inspiration to you, and I hope it reaches your heart—*m'lev el lev* מלב אל) (לב "from one heart to another"— from mine to yours. And I hope these pages inspire you to take action in your daily life so that you will have and continue to experience a satisfied heart for many days ahead. My wish is that this book serves as an opportunity to delve deeper into your *neshama*, or "your soul," for growth and recognition of self and others. May these words strengthen your key relationships through the examination of the deep and complex feelings we often have.

Chamber One

RELATIONSHIP TO SELF

What's in a Name?

The second book of the Torah, Exodus, starts with a portion called *shemot*, which means "names." The Exodus story begins with the naming of all the people who went down to Egypt. Why is this important? Why do I want or need to know all these names? After all, they mean nothing to me. But, as I reflect further on the power of our names, I recall *Midrash Tanchuma, Vayakhel* where our rabbis taught:

"אתה מוצא שלושה שמות נקראו לו לאדם: אחד מה
שקוראים לו אביו ואמו, ואחד מה שקוראים לו בני אדם,
ואחד מה שקונה הוא לעצמו; טוב מכולם מה שקונה הוא לעצמו."
"There are three names by which a person is called: the name
our parents call us, i.e., the name we are born with; the name
people call us; and the name we earn for ourselves. The name
one makes for himself is the best one of all."[1]

Do you have three names? Why did your parents give you your name? What do you do to make your name what it is? How do we live up to the name our parents gave us? Often, we are named after a person or a quality our parents want us to emulate. Have we done it? Do you feel proud of your name? Are there occasions where we are called names by others? Do you know what others call you? Do you agree with this name? Most importantly, how does one earn their own name?

In my Israeli military service, I was privileged to serve as an officer in a basic training boot camp. The training to become an officer was one of the hardest, yet most fulfilling, accomplishments because remaining in the course depended on my team's vote. How they viewed me and the name I gained through my actions served as a determining factor for my success. Later in life, while working with teenagers, I witnessed again how crucial is the name we create simply by behaving in a certain way. I had countless conversations with teens as well as adults regarding the importance of their actions as a true portrayal of who they are.

The rabbis concluded that the name we make for ourselves is the best one of all. What makes it best of all? The name we create for ourselves is the sum of all the actions we have engaged in throughout our lives. The good deeds we did, the interactions we had, and the conversations in which we took part.

With the hope that all of us desire to create a name for ourselves that will not only make us proud, but also be truthful to who we are, let's come up with a few thoughts and actions to illuminate the name we have chosen for ourselves.

Your Personal Lev Moment

1. If you do not know whom you were named after or for, do a bit of research. Why did your parents give you this name?

2. Ask friends and family you trust: What are the names they have given you? It will usually be adjectives that remind them of you. Ask them why they gave this name to you? How did you earn that name?

3. What name would you give yourself?

4. Using the concept "name" in the broadest sense (to reflect a person's identity), what are your three names? Which names would you want? What might you want your children's names to be?

5. What makes the name you have given yourself the best of all? When might it not be the best name of all? On what does it depend?

6. Explain the nature of your three names and observe their differences and similarities.

Where Are You Going?

I am always fascinated at how the Hebrew language conveys more meaning than meets the eye. The Hebrew language is a root-based language, meaning words in the Hebrew language are mostly constructed using three main consonants. Since there are a finite number of roots, there are many words that share the same root. This means words may be connected in a meaningful and particular way.

Let's take, for example, two words that share the same root, *conscience* and *compass*. In Hebrew, the word for conscience is *matzpoon*, written in Hebrew as מצפון. The word *matzpen* (מצפן), which means "compass," also shares the same root of three letters: *tzadik, pay,* and *nun (צ.פ.נ)*. By having the words *conscience* and *compass* share the same root, the Hebrew language is teaching us something very special.

What is a "conscience"? It is that inner voice or feeling telling us the direction of where we want to go, i.e., the difference between right and wrong. I truly believe human beings are born with this ability, the ability to know intuitively where they need to go, both spiritually and physically. Often, Jewish writings indicate that if you really listen to what your conscience whispers, you will know the correct next step to take.

Although in English these two words, *conscience* and *compass*, have nothing in common (at least not in their spelling), in Hebrew they are very much related. By using our *matzpen*, or compass, we can know the direction we are going, and if we follow our *matzpoon*, or conscience, we will arrive there safely.

Wait, there is more! This three-letter root also makes up the word that means "hidden," *tzafoon* (צפון). What does this all mean? What do these words have in common: *conscience*, *compass*, and *hidden*? Consider this: sometimes our conscience is hidden from us and sometimes where we need to go is hidden from us. Knowledge of having these three Hebrew words connected means that we need to work hard to uncover what is hidden in our lives and then bring this discovery to the surface so it can guide us.

Your Personal Lev Moment

1. Have you had a time in your life when you needed to go somewhere but your conscience resisted you? How did you convince yourself to do the right thing? Did you go to someone you trust to ask their advice? If a similar situation happens again, would you have a clearer direction?

2. Have you had instances in your life when you felt your spiritual destination, your soul destiny, was hidden from you? What happened that eventually shed light onto the situation? What did you do to find clarity? Did you pray for guidance? At what point did you leave it to the universe, or God, to show you the way? How did it feel to let go of your need to know and be in control?

3. This week, focus on the concept of your destination. What destination will make you feel you have used your compass and your conscience to make known all that is hidden to you right now?

4. Can you make peace with the idea of not knowing where you are going at times? Can you be satisfied living with situations that seem unclear? Can you hang out in a place that is unknown? How does it make you feel?

Focus on and nourish your conscience this week and make it a week in which you realize your direction, a week when the hidden will become revealed.

Know Your Roots!

I f you haven't figured out by now, I love the Hebrew language. No surprise, of course—I am, after all, an Israeli!

As I have mentioned before, Hebrew is a root-based language, meaning every word in the Hebrew language has three or four Hebrew letters that constitute its root. A combination of root letters can be shared in many different words, creating connection between words. This is something unique only to the Hebrew language.

Let's take another example I love—the word *masoret,* which in English means "tradition." The root for the word *masoret* consists of the three Hebrew letters *mem, samech,* and *reish* (מ.ס.ר). *Masar,* a word using the same three letters, means "pass forward." These two words, *masoret* and *masar,* share the same root, which shows a connection between them and creates an additional layer of understanding into the Jewish tradition. The traditions we have grown up with are what we

23

pass forward to the next generation, only for them to pass forward to the following one.

On the other hand, the word *kadima* in Hebrew, meaning "forward," consists of three Hebrew letters *kaf*, *dalet*, and *mem* (מ.ד.כ). These three letters also combine to form a Hebrew word that means "ancient"—*kadum*. So it appears that two words with seemingly little in common—*forward* and *ancient*—have some hidden connection. When we walk forward, we take our past with us. When we practice our traditions (those which have been practiced by our ancestors), we pass them forward to the future.

The more you learn Hebrew, the more you will love it!

Your Personal Lev Moment

1. What traditions do you pass forward to your family? From whom did you learn them? Why do you still practice these traditions? How do they reflect your values? Which ones make you feel most proud? When you pass your traditions onto your family, what is their reaction? What are the ways you pass them on? Does your family find the traditions as meaningful as you do?

2. Can you create a new tradition to pass on to your children?

3. Let me share one tradition that is meaningful to my husband and me. We love celebrating Passover. We love the traditions, the food, the story, the concepts, the theme, and the time of year we celebrate this holiday. When we were growing up, even though we enjoyed our own family's traditions, we wanted to create more meaningful experiences for our children. We modified our traditions a bit to better fit us so that we could pass them on to our children in more meaningful ways. Slowly, we incorporated more activities, stories, and songs. We even wrote questions which we sent to our guests

to contemplate before coming over. We purchased fourteen copies of our favorite *Haggadah* (a book that tells the story of the Exodus), which our guests use (every two get one, encouraging them to connect and socialize further). Every year we take pictures and later insert them into the books. At the end of the evening, our guests write comments in the book (or send us an email later that we print out and glue on the pages of the *Haggadah*). Our children already have conversations deciding who will take these *Haggadot* (plural of *Haggadah*) once we stop hosting the Passover Seder gatherings in our own home. If that is not passing on the tradition and the excitement to the next generation, I do not know what is.

I hope this inspires you to create your own tradition, one that future generations will be so glad to receive!

" כי שבע יפול צדיק וקם."
"For a righteous man can fall
down seven times and rise."
–King Solomon (Proverbs 24:16)

Is Change Inevitable?

I recently saw a sign proclaiming "Change is inevitable, growth is optional." How true is this! In order to make growth meaningful, we often need courage. In the past few weeks, I witnessed several people's courageous acts. My sister's behavior during her cancer treatment is the first that comes to my mind. When you think of courage, what comes to mind first? I recall hearing a sermon online from IKAR rabbis where they discussed physical courage vs. moral courage. What do you think is the difference? Most people think of physical courage, such as when people go to war and endanger their life to secure ours. Physical courage can also encompass other ways in which people save their fellow human—we see it in times of catastrophes. Physical courage is most evident when we need people to be leaders, and they step up. Can you think of a biblical figure who showed physical courage? Gideon? Samson? David? Their action are definitely one way of looking at courage.

What I am thinking about, however, is moral courage—the ability to make changes that will impact you and your family or community, without knowing the results and without seeing the outcome. Consider speaking up when it may not be the most admirable thing to do at that moment, when it sometimes means going against the tide of opinions and actions. We have all seen this in our daily lives and on the news. Can you think of biblical figures who showed us moral courage? Avraham and Moses come readily to mind!

The word for courage in Hebrew is *ometz lev* (אומץ לב). Interestingly, the word *ometz* comes from the same root as in the word "to adopt"—לאמץ! And the word *lev* means "heart." So we can look at courage as "adoption of the heart." What can your heart adopt? Perhaps new behaviors, new ways of looking at things, new opportunities?

I think moral courage is one of the hardest things we have to face if we want to grow and improve who we are because it inevitably asks us to change and challenge ourselves and to take a new path. Change can be very scary because we do not know what the outcome of the change might be. Not changing, on the other hand, can cause us to be stagnant and, at times, to regress from our abilities, our wishes, and our dreams. It can also lead us to be disappointed, causing us regret and embarrassment.

Recently, my oldest son showed moral courage in front of my youngest son. While walking in Brooklyn, they witnessed a man, full of rage, banging on a car of an older man and uttering anti-Semitic statements. My oldest son not only feared that the older man would be hurt, but he also could not stand idle by while witnessing anti-Semitism. He told the angry man to cool off and walk away. Things could have turned badly, but God protected them and nothing happened. While I was scared for their safety—I was also moved by my son's courage!

I once saw a T-shirt with a sentence I found meaningful: "Look back to learn. Look forward to succeed." My wish for all of us is to have the courage to do what needs to be done and thus experience positive and welcoming growth! Change is inevitable. Let's make growth—the product of change—something of which we can be proud!

Your Personal Lev Moment

1. Is there anything in your life that might need sprucing up—an imaginary injection of newness? Is there a plan you want to revisit, tailor, or tweak a little? Is there anything outside of your comfort zone you want to explore?
2. Who is your hero? Have they shown physical courage or moral courage? Are they alive? Why do you consider this individual your hero? What have they done to be impactful on you? Did their impact influence others besides you? Your family? Your neighborhood? Your community?
3. Can you think of a time or an action that caused change in you or in others?
4. Study a person from the Bible who showed either physical or moral courage. What about this individual drove them to demonstrate courage? What lessons do you glean from them?
5. Imagine you are wearing this T-shirt "Look back to learn. Look forward to succeed." Can you come up with two tasks you would love to succeed at? What is your plan of action to get you there? Can you begin with a couple of steps toward that direction this week?

Be a Champion in Your Eyes!

I marvel at the symbolism and the hidden meaning of the majestic Hebrew letters. All Hebrew letters are believed to have hidden facets of spiritual force within them. The first letter of the Hebrew language is *alef* (א). For now, I want to focus only on this letter—the letter *alef*. Every Hebrew letter has an equivalent numerical value. *Alef's* numerical value is one (and the letter *bet* is two, *gimmel* is three, and so on). The Hebrew word for "letter" is the word *ot* (אות). The word *ot* also means "a sign," implying that Hebrew letters, from *alef* to *tav*, have spiritual signs and energy force.

In the Talmud, it is said that Betzalel, who was tasked with the building of the Tabernacle in the wilderness, knew how to combine certain letters to form a word and thus create a physical manifestation of that word. In this way, he created the objects in the *Mishkan* (Tabernacle), which is why he was chosen for this holy task (*Brachot* 55a). What is inside these letters that makes them special?

Let's start with the name of this particular letter—*alef*. It shares the same root as the word *aloof* in Hebrew, meaning "champion" or "general."

Take a closer look at this letter's physical structure: א. *Alef's* formation is a combination of two other letters: a *vav* (a slanted single line: ו) and two *yuds* (shorter lines: י) stemming outward from the *vav* in opposite directions. The total numerical equivalent of this combination—one *vav* and two *yuds*—adds up to twenty-six (*vav* equals six, and *yud* equals ten, so two *yuds* is twenty). Twenty-six is also equal to God's holiest name. That name consists of the letters *Yud* (י), *Hey* (ה), *Vav* (ו), and *Hey* (ה) again (ten plus five plus six plus five).

This first letter of the Hebrew alphabet encompasses not only the unity of God, but also the essence of God in each one of us, which can be translated as the soul in each of us. What do I mean? Without this letter *alef* (א), there is no essence of godliness in us, nothing that makes our *neshama* (soul) uniquely us. So it is no surprise that *alef* (א) is the letter that appears in Hebrew words relating to the family unit, bringing God into each and every human being. All of us are known as "I" and are all connected to others: I (אני=*ani*), brother (אחי=*achi*), sister (אחותי=*achoti*), mother (אמא=*ima*), and father (אבא=*abba*). In addition, the letter *alef* appears in each personal pronoun: she (היא=*hee*), he (הוא=*hoo*), you (אתה=*atah*), we (אנחנו=*anachnu*), and so on.

What do we learn from this? We all have the godly gift of *alef* (א) inside of us. We all have the possibility of being a champion. How can you foster this idea in your life? How do you project it?

Your Personal Lev Moment

1. Do you believe you have a special spirit within you? How do you nourish your spirit? What do you do to fill your energy quota?

2. Do you let other people see your godly self in a way that is humble? How so?
3. How do you relate to your family when you realize they are all champions (אלופים) in their own way?

My blessing to all of us is that we will possess the ability to connect to our godly spiritual self and project it to everyone with whom we interact.

The Alef in YOU by Shirona

 "There are no problems, only opportunities for growth." [2] –Rebbetzin Dena Weinberg

Would You Choose Goodness or Kindness?

H as anyone ever told you that you are being too good? What does it mean to be "good"? How is goodness mentioned in the Torah? There are many instances where the word *tov* (good) is mentioned in the Torah. During the story of creation, God says at the conclusion of each day that it was good, *tov*. On the third day, God says *tov* twice.

How does goodness manifest itself in our lives? And how does Hebrew shed a light onto this concept and the difference between goodness and kindness?

"הגיד לך אדם מה־טוב ומה ה' דורש ממך כי אם־עשות משפט ואהבת חסד
והצנע לכת עם־אלוהיך."

"He has told you, oh man, what is good and what the Lord demands of you, but to do justice, to love loving-kindness, and to walk discreetly with your God" (Micah 6:8).

The word the prophet Micah is using is *chesed* (חסד). *Chesed* is translated as "kindness," not goodness. Isn't this surprising? The difference between the Hebrew word and the English translation encourages me to think deeper. What's the difference between these two words, *goodness* and *kindness*?

Is goodness a state of mind and kindness an action? Are people born kind and then choose to do good or step away from goodness? Or, is good finite, but kindness goes beyond what one thinks they can do even in their own minds?

Judaism advocates that goodness is the personality trait with which we are all born. Kindness is an action we choose to engage in, allowing us to influence our surroundings. Kindness does not remain with us, but spreads to others. This is demonstrated in the understanding that Moses was born *tov*, a state of being that does not involve others. In Micah 7:20, on the other hand, it is said *"V'titen chesed l'Avraham"*— "give kindness to Avraham." Avraham was given the ability to step outside of himself to create *chesed* in his environment. This is what *chesed* is all about: *Tov* versus *chesed*, *tov* and *chesed*. Be good, *tov*, and do *chesed*, kindness.

Your Personal Lev Moment

1. Can you recognize the quality of *tov*, goodness, in yourself? What about in others? Do you notice when you step out of goodness into *chesed*, kindness? Can you recognize this in others?

2. Over the years, I have come to realize that people with *chesed* are the ones who tend to become leaders, while people with goodness will more likely be good followers. Leadership requires taking initiative and being proactive—both

components of *chesed*—while goodness does not necessarily lend itself to taking care of anyone beyond the self.

3. Think of people in your life who have shown *chesed*. Think of people who have shown goodness. How do you think they cultivate their kindness and goodness and use them as a vehicle for kind actions? How do you measure yourself on this path of *chesed* and goodness?

Laugh! It's Good for You!

When was the last time you laughed at yourself?
Recently, during a family gathering on *Shabbat* with guests,
we found ourselves having a hearty laugh as we remembered
moments from the past. We remembered a rafting trip from twenty-
five years ago where one of our children fell into the water, as well
as a funny instance from the previous week in a restaurant where a
series of unfortunate events with the server caused us to finally get our
dinners an hour after ordering. We laughed at things we had done that
were either silly or funny. Boy, did we laugh! For twenty minutes, the
laughter around the table was contagious. We had new friends at the
table who had not experienced these funny situations, but nonetheless,
they joined in our laughter because they saw us laughing and thought
that was funny enough! At the end of our gathering, as our guests left,
they said the evening was one of the most memorable celebrations they

had attended, and they didn't remember the last time they had enjoyed a *Shabbat* family gathering to that extent.

Does this happen often to you? Do you just laugh for the sake of laughing? Recently, I attended a Jewish educators' conference, and there was an educator whose specialty was laughter sessions. At one of the dinner gatherings, she came onto the stage and instructed everyone to begin laughing from their bellies. At first, I thought this was quite odd, but I started with a smile and looked around me and saw other people smiling back at me. For some reason, I found this funny, so I started giggling. Before I knew it, I could not control my own laughter, and tears were coming out of my eyes. What an uplifting feeling—to laugh for the sake of laughter!

What was special about this experience? Clearly, the amount of laughter!

There are many quotes from our Jewish biblical sources that encourage laughter. Take, for example, the Book of Proverbs, known in Hebrew as *Mishlei* (משלי), where it is said, "A happy heart enhances one's brilliance, and a broken spirit dries up the bones" (17:22).

In Job (איוב), a book that questions the reasons and origin of personal suffering and God's role in it, we read: "Until He fills your mouth with laughter and your lips with shouting" (8:21).

Sarah, in the Book of Genesis, laughed when she overheard God informing her husband, Avraham, that a boy was to be born to them at the ripe old age of ninety-nine. I would be laughing, too!

While there is a debate about whether laughter adds years to your life, I truly believe, if nothing else, it will add life to your years!

Your Personal Lev Moment

1. Find reasons to laugh this week. Recall silly moments and begin laughing out loud.

2. Do you know laughter is contagious? Make a point this week to seek out opportunities that will make you laugh! Enjoy the laughter!

3. Choose to spend time with others whom you find funny. Watch movies or sitcoms (such as *Big Bang Theory*) and laugh away!

4. How about bringing laughter to someone today? You might be surprised to find that when a person laughs because of you, you will laugh in return!

Dorice and her family find the joy in laughter

Our *Neshama*—Different but All the Same

et's breathe. And let's breathe again. I feel my chest rising and falling, and I allow myself to deeply breathe. I let the *ruach* (רוח), or "air," of my breathing engulf my body, my inner organs, and I feel the air anchoring me down. My breath connects me to earth, to the ground below me. I breathe. I let air in, and then I exhale as though I am observing my own body from above. I try to think of nothing else. My mind is a blank slate, and for just a few moments, I feel emptiness.

In Hebrew, *neshima* (נשימה) is "breath." This Hebrew word always fascinates me because it shares the same root as the word *neshama* (נשמה), or "soul." The only difference is the addition of the small letter *yud* (י). In Genesis, we are told that when God created man, he breathed into his nostrils, and Adam, the first man, came to life. God is represented in the letter *yud* (ʾ), the letter that, when placed in the center of the word *soul*, becomes the word *breath*. When God enters our *neshama*, he enables us to take a breath, *neshima*. Simply put, when we allow God in, we can exist. We can live.

As Jews are known as people of the book, we have a tradition that began hundreds of years ago. As we read the many Jewish texts, rabbis, throughout the generations, wrote stories as a way of interpreting and highlighting a concept or a hidden meaning within a biblical text. We call these stories *midrash*.

I once heard a story about a time when God created human beings. He told the souls, who up to that moment were only in the company of the angels and God, they would have to go down to earth. The souls did not want to leave God, as they loved to be in the higher world, and they begged to stay. However, their objections were to no avail, as they were needed below. God promised they would not be tarnished, and therefore he would hide them in our human bodies. He would clothe the *neshama* with human flesh, and when we (humans) passed on, the souls would return to be with the Holy One, blessed be He. The souls had no choice but to obey God's command.

I think our task in life is to uncover the *neshama* that is within us, to know and to understand who we are and how we need to feed and nourish our *neshama*. This task will be ours from the moment we are able to think until the moment we rejoin our Creator. Although in English there is only one word for "soul," our sages say our soul actually has three elements, each one contributing a different dimension to the soul: *nefesh*—the physical side of our soul, the instincts; *ruach*—the emotional side and what creates our personality, our spirit, and our energy, the seat of good and evil; and finally, *neshama*—the intellectual and rational part of the soul.

Other sages commented that there are two additional dimensions: *chaya* (חיה), representing commitment and faith, and *yechida* (יחידה), conveying the unity of the soul and the essence of the soul. Over the years that I have spent teaching youth, I was always challenged with questions about animals. I recall telling my students that animals do not have souls, but humans do. I now understand that I was partly correct. Animals may have *nefesh* and *ruach*, but only humans have *neshama*!

I love the story of why God decided to put His breath into us through our nostrils to bring us to life. The angels asked God how He would bring a man to life. God replied, "Man has a few openings. Will I breathe into his ears? No, the ear hears gossip and unkind rumors. Will I breathe into his mouth? No, the mouth speaks *lashon harah*, or evil gossip and lies. Will I breathe into his eyes? No, the eyes see injustice and cruelty. I will therefore breathe into his nostrils."[3] The nostrils are the gatekeepers; outside particles that are not harmful can enter, but those that are harmful stay outside the body through the filtering system that naturally exists in our noses. Breathe in, inhale. Breathe out, exhale. Breathe in through your nostrils, bringing the goodness of God and the possibilities of tomorrow into your awareness. Breathe out the impure breath, the CO_2 and waste from our bodies. Exhale the unnecessary particles of today. Allow them to melt away, to become part of the past. Breathe in and look inward to the *neshama* God has bestowed in you, in each one of us.

In our morning prayers, we say that God has instilled in us a pure soul (*The Complete Artscroll Siddur*, p. 18). We are worthy of existence. We are here today. Let's focus on what is good in our life and let go of what could be harmful or toxic to us. Be thankful and grateful you are here, *today*. The present time is a gift. Today is a gift. Thank you, God, for giving me today.

Your Personal Lev Moment

1. Do you think your soul is hidden from you? How do you know what your soul desires?

2. Think of instances when you felt the different aspects of your *neshama* come to life.

3. Have you been feeling anxious? Do you believe in mindful meditation? If you have never experienced this, find a podcast, a class, a lecture, or a recording and follow for a few nights. Observe the difference that mindful meditation makes in your body.

4. What actions do you take each day that express your *neshama*? What makes you feel positive and good? Once you write this down, practice these actions for the next week. Your *neshama* will thank you!

"If you won't be better tomorrow
than you were today, then what
need do you have for tomorrow?" [4]
–Rebbe Nachman of Breslov

Counting the Days and
Taking Stock of Your Life

"למנות ימינו כן הודע ונביא לבב חכמה."

I n the Book of Psalms, we read, *"l'mnot yamenu."* ("למנות ימינו.")—
"So teach the number of our days, so that we shall acquire a heart
of wisdom" (90:12). What is the connection between valuing
our days and creating a wise heart? So many of us rush through our
days, busy and overwhelmed with life's tasks, obligations, and work.
We struggle to complete all of our obligations at work and at home,
rushing children from this activity to the next, and before we know it,
the day is over. We get into bed and rest just enough to start our tasks
and our responsibilities all over again the next day.

Let's press the pause button on our life for a second.

Wait. Breathe. Count to ten. Breathe again. Pay attention to this moment.

The word *l'mnot* (למנות) in Hebrew has two meanings. In addition to the meaning "to count" as it appears in this prayer, it also means "a portion," or *mana* (מנה). When Israelis buy a falafel (a yummy pocket bread with fried chickpea balls) in the market, they ask for *mana falafel,* which translates as "one portion of falafel." In essence, numbering our days is also indicative of "the portion" of our days. We are all given a set portion, a limited time on this earth. Choosing what to do with our portion will determine its quality. How is your day going to be? How are you going to make today meaningful? Once this day is over, it will not happen again. It may be a cliché, but that is why today is called "the present." Treat it like one. How would you treat a gift? Treat it gently. Go beyond today—how is your week going to be?

When God counted the Israelites time and time again in the Book of Numbers, many rabbis interpreted it to mean that God loves us so much he counts us several times, wanting to make sure no one is missing. What if we do the same thing with our days? Let's love our days. Let us not only count the days, but make every day count!

Your Personal Lev Moment

1. Record in a journal for one week. Each day, plan to do something that turns your day into a one-of-a-kind day—a unique, important, special day. It does not have to be something earth-shattering. It can be small. Write a reflection for each day, describing your experience. Describe how you are feeding your *neshama,* your soul. At the end of the week, review your progress and realize how you not only lived through a day, but made the day worth living.

2. When we value our days, we naturally value the important people who fill our days. Every day, make sure you connect

with one person you value. Ask them about their work and obligations, show interest in their life, and share about your life with them.

3. Describe in your journal or to a friend your vision of your life on this earth. What are your deepest wishes you want to accomplish during your lifespan? Can you take any aspect of this vision, small as it may be, and fulfill it this week? Taking one step at a time means accomplishing a long distance in your life.

" אם אין אני לי מי לי? וכשאני לעצמי,

מה אני? ואם לא עכשיו, אימתי?"

"If I am not for myself, who will be for me?

And if I am only for myself, what am I?

And if not now, when?"

–Hillel in *Ethics of the Fathers* 1:14

Knowledge Is Not Enough

ave you observed people behaving in a way that surprised you? Have you surprised yourself in the way you behave at times? Wisdom is not as easily accessible as one might think. A Jew has the opportunity to pray three times a day. In the middle of every Jewish prayer service there is a section called the *Amidah (עמידה)*, or "standing" prayer. Some people call this prayer *Shmoneh Esrei (שמונה עשרה)*, which means "eighteen," thus acknowledging the number of original benedictions in this section. Others refer to this section as *Ha-Tefilah* (התפילה), meaning "the prayer." The *Amidah* is considered to be the center of the Jewish prayer service.

In this prayer section, one of the things we pray for is *daat* (דעת), *bina* (בינה), and *haskel* (השכל)—roughly translated as knowledge, insight, and discernment (*The Complete Artscroll Siddur*, p. 102).

Why? Why is it not enough to ask only for knowledge? Or only discernment? Why insight? Here is my take on those three words and the progression I believe is needed to achieve complete wisdom.

Daat (דעת), or knowledge: This is the information, facts, and actuals in any given situation. This is what many of us learn first. Give us the information so we can discern from it what we need. *Bina* (בינה), or insight: This word in Hebrew shares the same root as the word *bain* (בין), which means "between." How is that helpful for us? For me, *bina* means that insightfulness is what you sense between the words, both those spoken and unspoken. Then comes the true reward—*haskel* (השכל), or discernment: Interestingly, this word shares the same root as the word *sechel* (שכל), which means "brains" or "common sense." *Haskel* is the third level of understanding—what we take from a situation, how we internalize the information, and how we project the new learning we just acquired. This is true growth!

Your Personal Lev Moment

1. Be humble in new situations. As Socrates said, "The only true wisdom is in knowing you know nothing." A friend recently shared with me an idea she learned from a podcast. The speaker said that he acted as if everyone is smarter than he is. Could you do this for one day? How does it make you feel?

2. Think before acting. Take as much time as you need to deliberate on a problem or a situation before deciding.

3. Learn from your mistakes. There is no shame in trying again after you fail.

4. Before making up your mind this week, ask yourself: Where do I learn my "stuff"? What do I discern from these facts I know? What am I learning for the future?

Our mind is a marvelous tool! Let's use it to make our life meaningful!

 "הפך בה והפך בה, דיכלה בה!"
"Turn it and turn it, for everything is in it!"
—Ben Bag Bag in *Pirkei Avot 5:26*

You Matter!

I was recently thinking about the commandment in Leviticus that instructs: "Love your neighbor as yourself" (9:18). Although we can discuss this commandment for a long time and from different angles, I want this particular *lev* entry to focus on the latter part of this statement—"as yourself." When we love ourselves, we are able to fully love and appreciate others. A person who has positive regard for themselves is able to communicate with others in a loving way.

Let's focus for a moment and ask what we love about ourselves? What do we bring to the world that causes others to love us? Perhaps I should call this not a *lev* moment, but a love moment. I have seen many people who do not love themselves enough, and I do not mean in a narcissistic way, but in a truly humble way.

When we love ourselves, it does not mean we have to be blind to our own shortcomings. However, I believe that when we accept who we are, we also allow growth to take place within ourselves.

Understanding that humans are not perfect individuals allows us to be able to love others because we would want others to love us. When we have a sense of personal well-being and accomplishment, then we can be more accepting, kind, and joyful toward other people.

There is a *mitzvah,* or "Torah commandment," in Judaism called *Bal Tashchit* (בל תשחית) which means "do not destroy." At first, when you think about this commandment, you might think we are instructed not to destroy the earth through pollution or lack of conservation. But many rabbis also refer to this *mitzvah* as the way we take care of our bodies, which is a borrowed gift from God. How we take care of our bodies shows our care for ourselves and our deep connection and responsibility to our well-being.

Let's make this coming week about loving ourselves and accepting who we are and, by doing so, loving others!

Your Personal Lev Moment

1. Go to the gym at least three times this week! Your body will love you. If you do not like the gym, go out for a walk. If you have a four-legged animal, take them with you! Rain or shine, your dog will love you, and you will feel great.
2. Make a healthy salad you have not made before.
3. Check out the new movies and treat yourself to one.
4. Forgive yourself this week if you forgot to do something.
5. Tell yourself: "I love me!"
6. Do one kind action toward another person. Do you feel rewarded? Do you feel better about yourself by doing small acts of kindness toward someone else?
7. Start every day by telling yourself, while looking in the mirror (although the mirror is optional), five things you love about yourself and your life. This practice helps keep things in perspective when the day starts to get away from you.

Wake Up

Have you ever heard a *shofar* blow? A *shofar* is made from a ram's horn and is an instrument Jews use for the High Holy Days. The tradition is to blow the *shofar* one hundred blasts during the Rosh Hashanah services. Some of the *shofarot* (plural of *shofar*) are short, and some are long and curvy. Traditionally, Jews from *Ashkenazi* descent (most associated with Eastern European Jewry) use the less-spiraled, shorter shofar, while *Sephardic* Jews (those from Spanish and Middle Eastern descent) use the longer and curvier *shofar*. All *shofarot* have one feature in common—they end in a swirl pointing upward, which symbolically represents a perfect vision of how hopeful our lives are. They are always facing up!

Let's concentrate for now on the sound of the *shofar*. The most similar sound I can think of is the trumpet, a sound that can be piercing, but also solemn. These sounds of the *shofar* definitely wake me up! Jews are invited to listen to the *shofar* during the month of

Elul, which is the last month of the Jewish year. What happens if you allow yourself to listen and reflect inward every time you hear the blast of the *shofar*? What will stir up inside of you? Judaism allows for us to engage in opportunities to be awakened, emotionally and spiritually, for the entire month of *Elul* and during the High Holy Days.

One year, I made a point of hearing the *shofar* every morning—for the entire month! This experience had a tremendous impact on me, even until this very day. Imagine you hear the sound of an ambulance every day at the same time. Will it pierce your heart? Will the sirens cause you to tremble? Will it cause you to worry? Will this sound cause you to be thankful that you are okay? Will it make you think of your own health? Will it make you think of others and wish them well? Perhaps you will be reminded to be more responsible for your health and make new decisions so you can live better? When I heard the *shofar*, the blasts made me think of all of these things.

In Hebrew, the word *shofar*, which means "to repair," consists of the three root letters *shin*, *pay*, and *reish* (ש.פ.ר). Coming from the same root, the word *l'shaper* means "to improve." When I hear the *shofar*, I listen to my inner conscience leading me to assess what I can do better. The deeply penetrating and reflective sound of the *shofar* and the Hebrew meaning behind the word help me to improve myself, to grow better as a human being, to know what I want in life, and to know what my soul desires. I hear myself and my conscience better.

I am reminded of Anne Frank's diary where she writes, "Parents can only give good advice or put them on the right paths, but the final forming of a person's character lies in their own hands."[5]

This is the same message the *shofar* conveys to me. For forty days—from the first day of *Elul* leading up to Yom Kippur—I think about refining my character and filling my life with more goodness.

Your Personal Lev Moment

1. For the next week, either in the morning or at night, take a few minutes to reflect on what happened in the past twenty-four hours that was good. Marvel at the goodness. Congratulate yourself for the good you have brought into the world. How did this goodness make you and others around you feel?

2. Does anything negative pop into your mind? In these circumstances, what can you do differently? Realize and acknowledge the feeling. Then, accept that it happened. Don't try to change or deny the feeling. Try not to fight with yourself that a mistake happened. Just acknowledge, internalize, and accept. This is the first step in loving who you are and filling your life with goodness!

3. What in life is an "alarm clock" for you? What do you do to re-evaluate your course of action? What keeps you on your toes to be the best that you can be?

May we be more aware of that which makes us better and stronger, and may we celebrate life by being present as we step through our lives.

"וַהֲסִירוֹתִי אֶת לֵב הָאֶבֶן מִבְּשַׂרְכֶם וְנָתַתִּי לָכֶם לֵב בָּשָׂר."
"And I will take away the heart of stone out of your flesh, and I will give you a heart of flesh."
(Ezekiel 36:26)

Chamber Two

RELATIONSHIPS WITH OTHERS

True Love Moment—Your First Love

D o you know what the first love mentioned in the Bible is? Was it Adam and Eve? After all, they are the first couple in the Bible. Was it Avraham and Sarah? They are the first Jewish couple, the beginning of our lineage. Perhaps King David and one of his wives? No, none of these are the answer! You might be surprised to learn that the first love discussed in the Bible is not between a man and a woman, but between a parent and his child. It is the love between Avraham and Isaac. In Genesis 22:2, God tells Avraham, "Please take your son, your only one, whom you love—Isaac—and go to the land of Moriah; bring him up there as an offering upon one of the mountains which I shall tell you." Wow! The first love is to your child. As much as we love our spouses, our strongest love is to our offspring. This love is unconditional. We coach them, educate them, parent them (nudge them, feed them, bug them to finish their homework and chores, etc.). Our children are our future.

According to the Talmud, one of the questions we are going to be asked when we meet our Creator at the end of our lives is "Did you have children?" (*Shabbat* 31a). I was surprised when I learned this. Why do you think this is? I think the answer is the true reason of why we are in this world. Each and every one of us (even those who do not have their own children) needs to leave a legacy when we depart this world—a society that is better off than when we were born. We want to leave the world better in terms of security, environment, peace, and opportunities! Our legacy—what we leave behind for the next generation—is crucial for us to consider and work toward while we are alive.

I am blessed to have children—three of my own and many others whose parents trusted me to influence and to teach the core values of Judaism. I saw their struggles as they became teenagers, witnessed their conflict with their friends as they learned to stand up for what they believed in, and counseled them to be the best they can be. Love is about giving from yourself. Love is about truly being present in their lives. My children are the instruments God placed before me so I can be the best I can be. For this, I am grateful beyond words.

Your Personal Lev Moment

1. How often do you tell your children and/or the important people in your life that you love them? How do you show your love? Is it only through material gifts? What kinds of gifts do you give? Are they meaningful, expensive, and/or fun? Would you consider changing them in light of the reading above?

2. Do you teach your loved ones what you value so they can continue your legacy? In what way do you follow up your words with actions?

3. If you do not have children, how do you leave your stamp on this world? Are you close with other people's children? Are they influenced by you? How does this make you feel?

" אמר מעט ועשה הרבה."
"Say little and do much; and receive
everyone with a cheerful face."
(*Pirkei Avot* 1:15)

For the Love of Family

I n February 2015, I went to Israel to visit my sister who had been diagnosed with an aggressive type of cancer. At the time, she was thirty-nine years old. I accompanied her to a chemotherapy appointment at a hospital in Tel Aviv. We entered the elevator to ascend to the third floor. My sister, who had lost all of her hair, covered her head with a large scarf. I also had a shorter scarf wrapped around my hair. A woman entered the elevator and bluntly asked if my sister's head covering was for religious reasons (a common practice for observant Jewish women). Straightforward questions are not out of the ordinary in Israel, where people speak their mind and are very forthright. My sister responded with a simple "no."

Interestingly, during that period of time in my sister's illness, I had the custom of wearing a head covering. People asked me as well if my head covering was for religious reasons. My answer always was "not exactly." At that time, being in the United States and living so far away from my sister, I felt that my head covering was a way to connect my being and my essence to my sister by recognizing her struggles. For me, this practice spiritually connected me to my sister, who lived 10,000 miles away, by remembering that she had lost her hair and was going through a dangerous time in her life. I made a conscientious decision that as long as she could not get a haircut (because she, in fact, had no hair), I would not either. If you have an opportunity to view the videos on my Facebook page *Lev Moments*, you will see me during that time in my life.

I am reminded of the ancient quote, "If I am not for myself, who will be for me? And, if I am for myself, who am I? And, if not now, when?" (*Ethics of the Fathers* 1:14). This is such a deep and rich verse with meaningful teachings for us all. What does it mean to be for someone else? When are we not for ourselves, but for other people? How does it make you feel when you are for other people? When in your life are you acting for your own self? Let's start thinking about this now. If not now, then when?

Your Personal Lev Moment

1. What do you do in life to keep yourself connected to others?
2. Think of a time when you put yourself on the back burner and someone else became a priority. How did this make the other person feel? How did you feel?
3. How often do we do what is comfortable and convenient? When do we conscientiously put forward efforts to make sacrifices that yield rewards to our community or loved ones? How does this make you feel?
4. Have you considered wearing a head covering for a week? Give it a try and observe the reactions and comments made by others. How does it make you feel?

Wearing a head covering during my sister's cancer treatment was my act of solidarity from afar while she was suffering through one of the worst times in her life. When her hair finally grew back, I uncovered mine as well!

The author is visiting her sister Bruria and accompanying her to her ninth chemotherapy appointment.

Friendship All Around You

"Let the honor of your friend be as dear to you as your own."
—(".יהי כבוד חברך חביב עליך כשלך")
"Yehee chavod chaveircha chaviv aleicha k'shelcha"
(Pirkei Avot 2:15).

Friendships: What an incredible and necessary asset to our everyday lives! Our friends pick us up when we are down and are honest with us when needed. Have you ever questioned how you are as a friend to other people? How do you honor your friends? Rabbi Soloveitchik commented on his deep relationship with the Rebbe, the Chabad-Lubavitch rabbi known also as Rabbi Menachem Mendel Schneerson, stating that even if they did not see each other for many years, they still had a strong bond.[1] Does this happen to most people?

For me, honoring a friendship is like honoring a good marriage. It requires give-and-take and open communication. Friendship means to put in the effort and show up in our friends' lives! I remember a moment I will cherish forever: I was experiencing a gloomy, dark day. I felt sad and unappreciated. And when I have moments like this, I tend to want to be home and get under the blankets. A friend called me to chat, and when I told her I was sad, she asked why. Before I knew it, the tears came rolling down my face. Within an hour, this precious friend was at my home with a piece of cake and tea. When she left, I felt so much better, even though the reason for my unhappiness did not change. But my perception changed. I was reminded that I have true friends with whom I can build a strong foundation as I grow older. I love this about my life!

I hope for you an awakening such as this—the realization that your friends care about you—and, with open communication and meaningful friendships, your blessings are numerous.

Your Personal Lev Moment

1. Call a friend today. Tell them how much you appreciate them in your life and how much they have added to your life and to the person you have become.

2. Celebrate with a friend! Sometimes life gets busy, and we become too engulfed in our daily/weekly/monthly tasks. We forget to pause and rejoice.

3. Let me share a story with you: A friend's daughter was getting married. Because the wedding was out of town, there would be more financial commitment, as well as time away from work to attend. Yet, without a lot of hesitation, I bought two plane tickets. Why? Because happiness is to be shared with others. Because joy is something that is precious. Because this is what makes life meaningful. On happy occasions, Jews toast with

the word *l'chayim*, which means "to life." This is because our tradition teaches us in a very subtle way that to have joy is to have life. So join in the celebration—you belong there!

"כי ה' יתן חכמה, מפיו דעת ותבונה."

"For the Lord gives wisdom; from His
mouth [come] knowledge and discernment."
(Proverbs 2:6)

Lead Away

I f there is one statement our children remember from their childhood, it is this: "Be a leader!" The leadership concept was one they were familiar with. My husband has been a leader with the local Jewish Federation for over twenty years, and I have been working and serving in our synagogue leadership. Growing up, I was a leader in my youth group and later on served as an officer in the Israeli Army. I quickly learned that it takes a lot of work to become a leader *and* stay a leader. Leadership, *manheegot* in Hebrew (מנהיגות), shares the same root *nun, hay,* and *gimel* (נ.ה.ג) as the word *driver*. To be a leader, a person must be the driver behind a cause and see it through by cultivating and mobilizing support from others.

But, at times, leadership can be lonely. I tell my students to imagine an equilateral triangle. The point of junction at the top of the triangle represents leaders. The base is wide, representing many people. As we climb up the leadership ladder, the space becomes narrower and narrower allowing for only a few people to be in the leadership position. The more you climb, the fewer the leaders on the top. I can understand why—leaders are often subjected to scrutiny above and beyond those who choose to stay and observe on the sidelines.

Judaism takes leaders very seriously. When Moses, the greatest leader of Israel, was overwhelmed with the tasks of single-handedly judging the people of Israel in the desert, he listened to his father-in-law, Jethro, and selected judges to alleviate his burden of responsibility. A leader must be humble enough to be open to suggestions and criticism. A leader cannot lead alone. They need support. Exodus 18:21 provides us the basics of who can be a leader (in this case, a judge). They need to be Good fearing people of accomplishment and of truth. Why these qualifications? Perhaps because leadership asks us to be for others first and then for ourselves. Being a leader cannot be for personal gain. Good leadership requires us to serve a higher purpose, a greater vision.

Moreover, when the people of Israel wanted to have a king rule over them, the prerequisite in the Torah was very detailed. In Deuteronomy 17:14–20, we learn that a king cannot have too many horses, wives, gold, or silver. More importantly, the anointed king must write his own copy of the Torah. Isn't this strange? What do you think happens to a person who is required to copy the words of Torah? I think the task makes him humble and increases his commitment to the greater good. By writing a Torah, one turns into a student—someone who constantly learns. When writing the Torah, a king must write every letter correctly or start over again. In other words, a writer of the Torah becomes acutely aware that they are God's messenger.

The same applies to leadership today. A leader's job is to pay attention to what it means to be of service—to convey God's message for the highest good. Good leaders want society to be better in the

future than it is presently. Strong leaders develop solutions to current
challenges and seek preemptive measures to potential problems. They
are the ultimate students. Good leadership means conducting ourselves
in a manner that builds a productive reality while not destroying
another's. How we guide ourselves, and the path we choose to take
determines our leadership quality.

I recall a particular incident I experienced as an education director.
A child's Bar Mitzvah took place on a lovely spring day. Since our
synagogue is located in a neighborhood by several upscale restaurants,
the family decided not to offer the customary lunch for the community
in the synagogue social hall but rather take only their guests for a
fancier meal. I chose to stay with the regular worshippers. My belief
was that we do not exclude any of the worshipers from a lunch,
regardless if they were invited or not. It was a decision that fit the
vision of the person I am, taking into consideration the congregants
I was serving. At times, a leader's decisions are difficult to make, but
these are the decisions that form the person you are—in your eyes and
everyone else's.

I invite you to leadership! It is more than the role you play—it's
the person you become.

Your Personal Lev Moment

1. Do you consider yourself a leader? If so, what qualities do you
   have that make you a good leader?
2. When you think of leaders in your community, what do you
   think is their gift? Do you support their vision? What is their
   higher purpose?
3. How do you foster leadership in your children? Your
   colleagues? Your community?
4. If you wanted to create a better tomorrow, what would be your
   first step?

5. If you are a leader in your community/organization, what would happen if you left tomorrow? Is there someone to continue your vision? How do you inspire the people around you?

6. Are you a good listener? Ask three individuals you work with or live with if they perceive you as an intentional listener. Don't challenge them when they answer. Accept their response and improve accordingly.

Be There for Each Other

I t is *Rosh Chodesh Elul*—the first day of the last month of the Jewish year. Since the Jewish year is based on the lunar calendar, the Jewish months are not specifically correlated with the Gregorian calendar. The month of *Elul* usually falls in August to mid-September. After a summer filled with outings, sun, and visits with friends, Jews begin to think about getting back into our regular routine. If you are a teacher, you begin to plan your year at school. If you are a student, you prepare to go back to school. If you are neither a student nor a teacher, you still prepare yourself for another season of beginnings. Endings and beginnings. Ending the Jewish year by beginning the last of the Jewish months, *Elul*.

Elul (אלול) is written in Hebrew with four letters: *Alef* (א), *lamed* (ל), *vav* (ו), and *lamed* (ל). The rabbis comment that this is an acronym for four Hebrew words: "*Ani l'dodi v'dodi li*" (אני לדודי ודודי לי).[2] This translates to "I am for my beloved, and my beloved is for me." In a world that values the self, what does it mean to be for someone else? Looking back at my own life, some of the most gratifying moments or highlights were my realization of my role as a friend, a wife, and a parent.

Our tradition teaches us that Moses ascended Mount Sinai on the first of *Elul*. Moses went up to receive the Ten Commandments, as well as the entire Torah, written and oral. He was there for forty days and forty nights, which, after simple calculation, indicates that he came down on Yom Kippur, known also as the Jewish Day of Atonement. While he was up on the mountain, the people of Israel were awaiting his arrival by fasting and praying. He returned on Yom Kippur (the tenth of *Tishrei*), a day when each one of us is being judged by God for our actions, deeds, and misdeeds.

What impresses me most about this story, however, is that this was not the first time Moses ascended Mount Sinai. This was his second time! The first time was on the Jewish date of the seventeenth of *Tammuz*. While Moses was away on top of Mount Sinai, the people of Israel sinned, and when he descended from the mountain and saw the people worshiping a golden calf, he smashed the tablets. Many people died, and the people of Israel were punished. What happened next is most revealing as to how to approach the month of *Elul*, the month that, according to Jewish tradition, is a time of reflection. *Elul* is a month when we measure our actions and missteps and commit ourselves to a more righteous path.

What did Moses do? He climbed back up. In a moment when he felt most defeated, he did not give up. He knew that to try again was his only choice. He successfully did what he had failed to do before. This inspires me and gives me hope! If we know we have wronged someone, we need to approach them and start a conversation to determine how we can do *teshuvah*, how we can seek forgiveness and return to our path by recognizing our wrongdoing. How can we turn around the situation to make a better outcome? It is equally important to acknowledge and express what we need from others. We are not alone—we have each other!

Your Personal Lev Moment

1. How are you serving as a friend, partner, and/or parent? How do you help strangers? Sometimes how we treat those we don't know speaks more about us than how we treat those we know.
2. How do you pick yourself up and regroup if you have wronged those who are dear to you? Do you think the month of *Elul* will be a good time to approach those with whom you have had a falling out?
3. In case you read this entry any other time of the year—how about practicing *teshuvah* throughout the year? Would you consider trying to amend wrongs without waiting for the "perfect time"? Or can you set a time, for example, at the end of each month and make amends?

May the month of *Elul* this year be a *chodesh tov*—a good month! May this month (or any month) bring resolution to be a better friend, better spouse, better parent, and better citizen of the world.

"הַחֲזֵק בַּמּוּסָר אַל תֶּרֶף נִצְּרֶהָ כִּי הִיא חַיֶּיךָ."
"Take fast hold of discipline, do not let it loose, for it is your life."
(Proverbs 4:13)

Judge a Person Favorably

Isn't it true that most of us, if asked, would say it is not our place to judge other people? When asked, we would say we cannot accurately judge because we cannot be in someone else's shoes, which means we cannot judge someone else unless we have similar circumstances to theirs.

Our Jewish tradition actually says something different. Stick with me for a moment here.

In *Ethics of the Fathers*, a book which teaches us the codes of Jewish life, we read "Judge a person favorably"—"והוי דן את כל האדם לכף זכות" (*Pirkei Avot* 1:6). What does this mean?

I think we can safely assume that all of us have been in this place of judging others or being judged by others. I heard a story of a poor family who had a daughter who was about to be married. But the family had no money, so friends and family helped by donating money to create a special celebration. Each family donated as much as they

reflecting on your face in the mirror. Try to express a more forgiving look. It is a fact that when you smile, the mere lifting of the corners of your mouth can actually make you feel better about yourself and your situation, even if you start off by faking the expression. Try this for yourself. What do you have to lose?

3. Using the same mirror, look again at yourself. Be truthful and candid. Are you letting people define you, your personality, or your character by what they say? Are you living up to the person you were meant to be? Try not to hold a grudge; instead, know your value and live up to it.

Your attitude is solely up to you. It comes from you, and it reflects you. You determine your attitude. Recently, I noticed a sign saying "Attitude is contagious. Is yours worth catching?" Are you true to whom you want to be? If not, challenge yourself to come up with three new ideas to get you there!

" כי טובה חכמה מפנינים וכל–חפצים לא ישוו לה."
"For wisdom is better than pearls; all desirable things cannot be compared to it."
(Proverbs 8:11)

Wisdom Is Not Only up to Me!

E thics of the Fathers (*Pirkei Avot*) is part of the Talmud, one of the ancient books in Judaism—a book which addresses ethical codes for daily living. In it, Ben Zoma (a Jewish sage who lived in the first and second centuries CE) asks, "איזהו חכם?"—"Who is wise?" and answers, "הלומד מכל אדם."—"The one who learns from everyone" (4:1). Do you agree?

What have you learned from other people? Do you tell a person that you have learned something from them? Do you acknowledge that this person might know something you do not?

Other sages similarly asked, "Who is wise?" But they answered a bit differently than Ben Zoma. They replied, "The one who sees the outcome of his deed" (*Kedoshim*, *Tamid* 32a). If you were to discern what kind of wise person you are or strive to be, what would you conclude? Would you follow Ben Zoma or the other sages? Do you learn from your own mistakes? If not, how often in life do you allow yourself to learn from others? When we do learn from others, do we give them their due credit—the credit for being our teachers? We are wise when we are able to adjust our behavior based on the wisdom of others.

Our sight is an important tool in determining the consequences of our behavior. As parents and adults, our children, our colleagues, and our friends see our behavior and learn from our actions. We model who we are by the behaviors we exhibit. Our actions speak as loud as our words and make a longer lasting impression. We make judgments about what we see others do, and others make judgments based on what they see in us. What kind of wisdom do you incorporate into your life? Do you use your own wisdom to predict how you will impact your decisions today? In my old office I had a well-known quote (Talmud, *Ta'anit* 7a, spoken by Rabbi Yeshua ben Levi) painted on a wall:

"מכל מלמדי השכלתי ומתלמידי יותר מכולם."—"I have learned much from my teachers, but from my students I have learned the most." And I truly did.

As Moses delivered his last speech to the Israelites in the desert, he shared with the people the final words God spoke to him: "See. I give before you today the life and good, the death and bad" (Deuteronomy 30:16). We have the ability to see the results of our actions, my friends. It comes in the form of the goodness around us, the acknowledgment from others to us and from us to others. So let's make this time full of wisdom. May we see the fruit of our labor.

Your Personal Lev Moment

1. Follow Ben Zoma's recommendation to learn something new from another person this week (a friend, your student, an employee, or even your child). Give them credit for being your teacher.

2. Can you think of your past actions and how they shape who you are today? Think of two examples. What actions would you take that will make you proud a year from now?

3. If you were to give advice to your younger self, what would it be? Do you like who you have become?

4. Which trait do you believe is the most important one to have in order to be able to learn from others?

Judgments and Perception

It is four in the morning, and I am flying to Philadelphia through Phoenix. I have no make-up, my hair is in a bun, and I'm wearing my glasses because, let's face it, who am I going to impress at this early hour of the day? Next to me sits a man who looks younger than me. His pants are torn. His sweatshirt is a bit dirty. He has a ponytail, and he smells of cigarettes. Not horrible, but I can still smell it. He tells me he is traveling because his "old lady" is having a baby. He has a deep southern accent. I start making assumptions. I can feel it. He probably is poor; he has nothing; he is a no-good kind of a guy.

Since I have no TV monitor in front of me, I think to myself, "Okay, Dorice, don't make assumptions. Have a conversation with this man." For the next couple of hours, he opens his heart to me. (I don't know what it was about me that made him reveal so much—it must have been the glasses I was wearing.) I learn he has a wife; he is in his third marriage; she came to the marriage with three children; and this is their first child together. I learn he lost a child in his previous marriage. I learn he was heavily addicted to drugs three years ago but quit when his son died. And I learn we do not share the same opinions about politics. We share almost nothing in common. I learn that what keeps him away from drugs is his strong will to make his marriage and his life better than the one he was handed growing up.

During our conversation, I begin to feel compassion for a man who has had so many struggles in his life. Although I had thought he might be extremely poor, I learn that he makes double what I make by installing environmental pipes. First lesson of the morning: Never make assumptions about what you don't know. There is a Jewish proverb that tells us

"אל תסתכל בקנקן אלא במה שיש בו."—"Don't look at the vase, but what it has inside of it" (*Ethics of the Fathers* 4:27). The "cover" of the man in front of me may be tattered and bruised, but the inside is excited and looking forward to a new life for himself and his "old lady."

As we land in Phoenix, he asks me what he should learn and read tonight in the Bible. I think for a second, and then I recommend Leviticus 19. (If you question why I chose that verse, read to find out why that was my recommendation.) As we depart, he says, "I will forever remember you from this flight." I certainly have remembered him!

On my next flight, a woman sits next to me. She is around five feet seven inches and looks gorgeous. Assumptions are being formed. (I think: she makes good money, is happy, and has her life figured out.) We start chatting, no surprise to anyone who knows me. I learn she is a TV personality in the sports industry. She tells me about how much effort is needed to keep up her body and her looks because that is "what sells." She opens her laptop to show me some of her work, and that is when I glance over at a picture in the background where it appears that she is extremely bruised. I ask, "What is that? How did this happen?"

She replies, "Oh, this was the plastic surgeon's work because I have to look good for the TV. I have him on my speed dial." Then she reaches over and grabs a bag of pills.

Now it will not surprise you one bit to hear that I asked, "What are all these vitamins?" She looks at me, smiles secretively, but doesn't respond. I think to myself: "Don't assume, Dorice. Don't judge."

It didn't take me long to realize that, on both flights, I made assumptions about the person sitting next to me, and both were wrong. Do you sometimes make assumptions? Do you sometimes judge others? Do you realize when you are doing this? I think human beings have the tendency to place people in particular boxes because it makes our lives more organized. In truth, assumptions never prove to be a healthy way of living life.

I am reminded of a blessing we say every morning: "אשרינו מה טוב חלקנו, ומה נעים גורלנו, ומה יפה ירושתנו." "How fortunate we are, how good is our portion, how pleasant is our lot, how beautiful is our heritage!" (*The Complete Artscroll Siddur*, p. 26).

No judgement. Gratitude instead. We are happy with our lot!

Let's enjoy the weeks and months ahead without making assumptions about others. We never know what is in store for our lives!

Your Personal Lev Moment

1. Recall an assumption you made. What was your "wake-up call" to resist and perhaps reject this assumption?

2. Have you heard assumptions made about you? How did it make you feel? How did you respond?

3. Do you like to have conversations with people you do not know when you are traveling? Or do you tend to keep to

yourself? How would you like people to approach you? How do you let them know your preference?

”שמע עצה וקבל מוסר למען תחכם באחריתך.“
"Hearken to advice and accept discipline, in order that you may be wise in your later years."
(Proverbs 19:20)

What We Have Is Enough

P lease let me share a story my mother told me: Once there was a king who wanted to throw a party for all his subjects. He conversed with his advisors to create the best party. Hundreds came to the party. They drank, ate, and danced and had a fabulous time all night long! When the king saw how successful the party was, he told his advisors to give each person a sheep on their way out as a gift from him. As he sat on his throne by the window, he saw that all his guests left with a sheep of their own, and he was happy. But, alas, what he did not hear were the words of the people leaving his palace with their sheep, looking at each other and saying, "How inconsiderate of the king—he gives us a sheep, but how can we properly leave if he doesn't bother giving us a leash?"

This story makes me think of the great black hole into which many of us get sucked. When is what we have, or what we receive, enough? There is a Jewish holiday, Passover, that takes place in the spring with a tradition that calls on us to clean our homes of *chametz*, which traditionally refers to any leavened food. Figuratively, *chametz* can refer to the extra things we don't necessarily need in our lives. For many Jews, spring cleaning is Passover cleansing—getting rid of that which holds us down and instead appreciating what we have and what we receive.

How do we make the existing realities in our lives enough for us to be thankful? When do our expectations become a barrier to our ability to live in the moment and be joyful? In a few pages, you will read a story of generosity from a complete stranger that made my day so much more pleasant. This experience was so significant I decided to include it in this book. What I take with me today is not to value a gift by the "leash" with which it is given, but by the heart that was put into it.

Your Personal Lev Moment

1. Try to recall a time when you were given something that filled your heart with joy. Try to relive this feeling. Was your feeling the result of the size of the gift or the thought that went into it?
2. Think of one example of a gift you have given. What was your motivation in giving? What did you want your recipient to feel?
3. What do you have in your home that you do not need but others would value? Can you give something away?
4. What are ways you can cleanse your soul and your expectations from what is not needed—from what clutters your vision as well as your home?
5. Focus on being appreciative for all the things others do for you! Verbalize it!

"אור זרע לצדיק ולישרי לב שמחה."
"A light is sown for the righteous,
and for the upright of heart, joy."
(Psalms 97:11)

Circumcision of the
Heart Needed for All

"וּמָל ה' אֱלוֹהֶיךָ אֶת לְבָבְךָ וְאֶת לֵב זַרְעֶךָ לְאַהֲבָה
אֵת ה' אֱלוֹהֶיךָ בְּכָל לְבָבְךָ וּבְכָל נַפְשְׁךָ לְמַעַן חַיֶּיךָ."

In the Book of Deuteronomy, it is said, "*HaShem*, your God, will circumcise your heart and the heart of your offspring, to love *HaShem*, your God, with all your heart and with all your soul, that you may live" (30:6). What does this mean? How can a heart be circumcised? What does circumcision have to do with loving?

Before I answer, did you know that according to Jewish wisdom, the first man, Adam, as well as Moses, were born without foreskin? And did you know that only after he ate from the Tree of Knowledge did Adam develop an *orla,* the foreskin that is traditionally removed during a circumcision ceremony?[4]

Jewish tradition advocates that when we are born, we are born pure. Our hearts are pure without any blemish. As we grow, we learn behaviors that are not positive for our souls and do not contribute to our holy selves which causes us to become desensitized to how we treat others. We figuratively grow another layer of skin so that we do not feel the impact of our words and actions on others. At the moment when the extra layer of skin has grown, God interrupts and circumcises the part that is not necessary for our being, thus bringing us to our original self, to a pure state.

If the circumcision vision is hard for you to grasp, how about this vision: imagine yourself as a vessel. You are a beautiful, clear glass vase. As we grow and mature, our clear vase gets dusty—dusty because it was outside, because we filled and emptied the vase several times. It develops a layer of film that makes the glass less clear. There are stains. It is not as shiny as it once was. But then we wash the vase in warm soapy water. What is the result? A beautiful vessel, as clear a vase as the moment it was created. This vase is like our heart. How does our heart get "dusty" or "grow another layer"?

I believe most of us are people with honorable intentions. But, at times, all of us make mistakes by not using our words the way God intended, by not being sensitive to others and their needs, by talking more than listening, by taking more than giving, by criticizing more than complimenting, and by hating more than loving. We grow dusty. I am sure you can think of more ways our hearts can become dusty. But then God comes and "circumcises" our heart. Once he does, we are able to love! Our channels of goodness, kindness, love, empathy, and so much more are once again open.

Your Personal Lev Moment

1. Are there times when you feel you are not living up to your best self? What do you think are the reasons for this feeling?

2. What actions do you think you can take to elevate your heart so that you can sing and rejoice?

3. In the world we are living in today, what do you regard as the three most important traits we, as humanity, need to regain so we can live the best life possible? As a nation, as a people, and as an individual? Which one trait must we rid ourselves of?

Enough Blessings to Go Around!

Here is a fun, spiritually-elevating activity that will cause your heart to grow exponentially! Gather a group of people for a fun, social evening. Provide a small piece of paper and a pen for each participant. Have everyone write a blessing and a wish to themselves. Instruct them to write the blessing in first person. Fold each paper in two and place it in a jar and place the jar at the center of a table. Then have each person take a random piece of paper from the jar, read the blessing aloud, and share how this blessing (most likely written by someone else) is beneficial and meaningful to them.

I have done this activity several times with different groups, and in each gathering, the individuals were so delighted to receive their blessings, even though it wasn't what they wrote for themselves initially. If you were taking part in the activity, would you take your own blessing for yourself, or would you rather open your mind to a blessing written by someone else?

When I shared this activity with my daughter, Hadas, she said it reminded her of the idea that if everyone placed their particular life journey in a pile and stated it, and then everyone had the opportunity to take their path back or switch with someone else, they would almost always take back their own journey. Even though we say, "I would much rather have that person's life than my own," when push comes to shove, it just takes a little appreciation for how blessed you really are to remember that your life is good! Isn't it true?! But with blessings, this is not necessarily so.

Sometimes we can benefit more from other people's blessings. One morning, a wonderful thing happened. I was in my car in a line for my weekly treat of a blended iced coffee. There were about six cars in front of me, and it took about ten minutes before my car was at the window to purchase my drink. When I drove up, I rolled down my window and handed over the money, only to find out the person before me had paid for my drink!

This small act of kindness not only took me by surprise, it illuminated my frustrations and impatience. I immediately felt blessed the entire day. Why? Because someone I didn't know did something kind to someone they did not know. That feeling of kindness stayed with me the entire day and colored my perception in a very positive light. This was definitely a blessed moment.

Here is a Hebrew gem to increase your enjoyment: Do you know that the Hebrew word *bracha* (ברכה), translated as "blessing," is very similar to the word *breicha* (בריכה), which means "a pool of water"? They both share the same Hebrew root *bet, reish,* and *chaf* (ב.ר.כ). Our blessing is a source of water, engulfing us and penetrating into our very being. It is no surprise that many faiths and traditions use a body of water to ritually and spiritually cleanse our being. May all the blessings wash over your body like water, and may you feel the blessings soak into your body, satisfying and nourishing you from the inside out.

Your Personal Lev Moment

1. What are the blessings in your life? Each day, think of a different reason why on that specific day you are blessed. Write this down. I have found when I write something down, it becomes even more real and obvious to me. Within a week, you will have a collection of blessings.

2. Here is an assortment of *brachot*, blessings, in case you have a gathering and want to skip the first step in the activity I described above:

    I am blessed to have health in my life.

    I am blessed to travel to interesting places.

    I am blessed to have stability in my life.

    I am blessed to have opportunities in my life.

    I am blessed to overcome my fear of the unknown.

    I am blessed that I have this hobby.

    I am blessed to be able to do ____.

    I am blessed to feel accomplished.

    I am blessed to have the support of a special person in my life.

 "אילו פינו מלא שירה כים."
"Were our mouth as full of song as the sea."
(*The Complete Artscroll Siddur*, p. 400)

Chamber Three

RELATIONSHIP WITH GOD

Love and Then Some More Love!

"Hear, O Israel, the Lord is our God, the Lord is One."
"You shall love the Lord your God with all your heart, with all your soul, and with all your might. And these words which I command you today shall be upon your heart. You shall teach them thoroughly to your children, and you shall speak of them when you sit in your house and when you walk on the road, when you lie down and when you rise. You shall bind them as a sign upon your hand, and they shall be for a reminder between your eyes. And you shall write them upon the doorposts of your house and upon your gates" (Deuteronomy 6:4–9).

This prayer (*Shema V'ahavta*) is one of the most important prayers in the Jewish tradition, which is the reason I chose to put it in the very first entry of the third chamber—our relationship to God.

Taken from the last book in the Torah, Deuteronomy, these words express the main essence of Judaism and are sung in every

Jewish prayer service. The *Shema* is the oldest fixed daily prayer in Judaism. Unlike spontaneous prayer, where people are emotionally and spiritually moved to pray in whatever form they choose, this fixed prayer, the *Shema*, followed by the *V'ahavta* ("You shall love the Lord your God…"), is sung multiple times a day.

After reading the English translation of the *V'ahavta* prayer, a question arises: How can we be commanded to love God? In what ways are we living this and transferring this love to our children, students, colleagues, families, and community?

Let's look deeper at the first line: "Hear, O Israel, the Lord is *our God*, the Lord is One." The plural is indicated by the Hebrew word *Eloheinu* (our God). Compare this to the beginning of the paragraph of the *V'ahavta*: "You shall love *your God* with all your heart." The Hebrew word *Eloheichah* is used and is singular for "your God."

Why this difference? I believe our rabbis are teaching us a powerful lesson. While acknowledging that God is *our* God, there is a recognition that love is a very subjective concept. No two people show their love the exact same way, nor do they feel love in the same way. When I recite this prayer, I sense its encouragement to look inward (hence the tradition of the initial action of covering our eyes while saying the first line) and to observe my feelings and my connection to *HaShem*, God. How do I love? How do I show love? Is there something I need to improve to better show love? The prayer requires us to love God with all our **heart**, all our **soul**, and all our **might**. In which of these three ways do I show my love to God? Is it only through my heart? How do I express this? Or do I show love through my soul, and if so, how does that manifest itself? Or is it in my actions, my might, with all that I have? How do we show love using all three manifestations of expressions of our love to God?

Your Personal Lev Moment

1. Years ago, I read *The 5 Love Languages* by Gary Chapman.[1] Within its chapters, the author describes the five ways to show love: gift giving, quality time, words of affirmation, acts of service, and physical touch. Would you consider experimenting with other forms of showing love? Have you ever asked your "love recipient" for their preferred ways to be shown love? What way do you show love toward God?

2. Would you use any of these five ways? Describe your feelings and your actions—why do those actions express your love?

3. What can we learn from the way we love *HaShem* and apply that to how we love our family? Or vice versa?

4. If you do not know the *Shema V'ahavta* but want to learn it, here is the prayer in both Hebrew and transliteration in English. Begin reading each word slowly, concentrating on the phonetic pronunciation.

"שמע ישראל ה אלוהינו ה׳ אחד. ואהבת את ה׳ אלוהיך בכל לבבך ובכל נפשך ובכל מאודך. והיו הדברים האלה אשר אנוכי מצווך היום על לבבך. ושננתם לבניך ודברת בם בשבתך בביתך ובלכתך בדרך ובשכבך ובקומך. וקשרתם לאות על ידך והיו לטוטפות בין עיניך. וכתבתם על מזוזות ביתך ובשעריך."

Transliteration:

"*Shema Yisrael, Adonai Eloheinu, Adonai echad. V'ahavta eit Adonai Elohechah, b'chol l'vav'chah, u'v'chol nafsh'chah, u'v'chol m'odechah. V'hayu had'varim haeileh, asher anochi m'tzav'chah hayom, al l'vavechah. V'shinantam l'vanechah, v'dibartah bam b'shiv't'chah b'veitechah, u'v'lecht'chah vaderech, u'v'shoch'b'chah u'v'kumechah. U'kshartam l'ot al yadechah, v'hayu l'totafot bein einechah. U'ch'tavtam, al mezuzot beitechah, u'vish'arechah.*"

"Prayer is the service of the heart."
(Talmud *Ta'anit* 2a)

Ahh—It's Finally Here

T here is one day of the week I always look forward to experiencing.
During my childhood, the entire household worked to get
ready for this day. My mother would begin the preparation on
Wednesday or Thursday morning with baking. I would come home
from school, and the smells of rugelach, a type of chocolate cake,
would greet me at the door. Thursday afternoon meant my sisters and
I would help my mom with cleaning, chopping vegetables, and going
to the store for last-minute shopping to buy any items my mom forgot
during her earlier trip to the market. On Friday afternoon we would be
setting the table, and then the day would arrive—the Sabbath, known
in Hebrew as *Shabbat*, the day of rest. This was a day I cherished.

Even though my father would go to synagogue every Friday
evening, the girls stayed home. We would paint our nails and then
light the candles and wait for the men to return. My mom would stand
for a few minutes by the candles after they were lit, whispering silent

prayers from her lips to be heard only by God: words of appreciation, words of acknowledging *Hakadosh Baruch Hoo*, "Blessed be He," and words asking God to protect her children. A holy and sacred moment that was, and still is, special for me as I light my own candles, decades later. Friday night growing up meant no one was going out to parties. It meant sitting together around the table, singing songs, eating the best food of the week, and enjoying each other's company. Saturday morning meant reading novels while waiting for my dad to return from synagogue and then having our special *chamin*, a Persian *cholent* (a slow cooked dish traditional to many Jewish households), a dish that had been cooking on a hot plate since the evening before.

As I grew up and then had my own family, I continued the tradition of getting ready for this day with enjoyment and anticipation. We often have guests come and join us for the *Shabbat* meal. My family's favorite foods are always made on *Shabbat*. My mom's Persian cooking is duplicated in my kitchen, and when my husband enters the house on Friday afternoon, his first words are "Ahh. It's the smell of *Shabbat*."

On *Shabbat* mornings I often go to synagogue now. I have discovered and am immensely grateful for the egalitarian aspects of my life. I not only learned the prayers and their importance, I am now helping to pass them onto the younger generations. I have learned to read Torah (the first five books of the Bible) as well as *Haftarah* (a portion chanted each week from the later books of the Bible). I cherish the ability and the right for any Jew to participate in the service in any way that shows their knowledge and commitment, regardless of their gender. At the same time, I value that there are different streams of thoughts within Judaism, thus every Jew can find their *kehillah*, or "community," and have a meaningful experience. This day is the highlight of my week.

What is so special about this day?

The word *Shabbat* in Hebrew comes from the root "to cease"—to stop and pause from our everyday life and just appreciate what is. All week long, beginning on Sunday (just as it is the first day of the creation, it is also the first day of the week), we do what we need to do for our lives: work, chores, and meeting obligations. But on *Shabbat*, the seventh day, we nourish our *neshama*, our soul. We don't worry about working or creating, only enjoying what has been created thus far.

The root of the word *Shabbat*—*shin, bet,* and *tav* (ש.ב.ת)—is also shared with the Hebrew word *shvita* which means "strike." *Shabbat* is a day when we do not perform our regular tasks. It is also no coincidence that the Sabbath is the seventh day of the week (not the fifth, sixth, etc.). The number "seven" in Judaism is a special number, a number that signifies a completion and an elevated status. A bride circles her groom seven times during the marriage ceremony. There are seven weeks between the holidays of Passover, when we secured our physical freedom upon leaving Egypt, and Shavuot, when we received the Torah on Mount Sinai, thereby acquiring the spiritual freedom and the road map to living an ethical life.

The Sabbath is a day we need so that our week ahead can be full of vigor and creativity. It is a day to "unplug," a day when we take time to enjoy our friends and our family. *Shabbat* is a day when a busy parent can be fully devoted to their children without worrying about being on social media or meeting a work deadline.

Shabbat is not only an "Ah-hah" moment, but an "Ah-hah" day! The seventh day. *Shabbat* begins on Friday at sundown and ends Saturday night when you see three stars in the sky. If you have not tried, I challenge you to give the *Shabbat* experience a chance. It may give you much more than you bargained for!

Your Personal Lev Moment

1. If you have never experienced *Shabbat*, begin easy. Plan a fun, family dinner around the table and follow it up with board games, storytelling, and social time. No TV, iPads, laptops, or phones—just the company of your own voices. How does it feel? You may need to do this for several weeks to get the hang of it. Next, invite another family to share a Friday evening with you. If you are inclined, recite the blessing over the candles, wine, and bread before partaking in the meal. Make the meal intentional. What do you want to achieve out of this gathering?

2. To fully appreciate *Shabbat*, try to carry some of the holiness of Friday night to the Sabbath day. If you are open to experiencing religious services, find a place that suits you and your family. Perhaps meet the religious leaders beforehand to see if they have programs that would fit your family. Greet the day with intention by giving emphasis to your clothing and your appearance, as this is different from going to a regular fun outing at the movies. Try this for several weeks. At first, this extra focus might feel like a task, but before you know it, this practice will be a pleasure that will nourish your soul for the rest of your life.

3. If you are not Jewish but curious about this one-day pause in the week, approach Jewish people and see how they celebrate *Shabbat*. Perhaps join them for a Friday night celebration?

4. Can you carry any aspect of *Shabbat* into another day of the week? Could you set aside a day of no screen time? Could your family have a day for playing games together?

5. Find *Shabbat* music on YouTube, Spotify, or other music apps. It is sure to get you in the mood for something special!

"More than Jews have kept *Shabbat,*
*Shabba*t has kept the Jews."[2]
–Ahad Ha'am

You Can Be What You Eat!

Years ago, when I came to the United States, I was invited to share meals in people's homes. I was a foreigner, and this was a very kind gesture from my new friends. My English was not good; I was not comfortable with the American culture; and I did not know many people. It all felt so new. Coming from a strictly kosher home, I was shocked to see that many of the hosts, who graciously invited my husband and me, were not keeping kosher. Examples included a Mexican meal of ground beef with cheddar cheese, a lamb hamburger with a glass of milk by its side, and even shark kabobs on a stick. While for many people this would be a delicious meal, it alerted me to a decision I would have to make. Do I join the meal festivities and forget about this "small" restriction of Judaism, or do I keep true to who I am by choosing the food I eat? I chose the latter. I chose once again to be a minority in my community. I chose to teach my children (and subsequently my students) how to follow the laws of *kashrut*. I chose to eat dairy or selected fish when people invited us over. I decided to make it easy on everyone and tell them that, outside of the house, I am a vegetarian. And this has been working out for me thus far!

The concept of *kashrut* as a *mitzvah* (in this context, *mitzvah* means "commandment" rather than "good deed," as it often is translated), comes from the Torah. In Leviticus 11 and in Deuteronomy 14, we read about the forbidden foods to avoid. From this, our Jewish sages derived the rules of what is kosher to eat and what is not. The phrase "Do not cook a kid in its mother's milk" is mentioned in the Torah three times—twice in Exodus (23:19 and 34:26) and once in Deuteronomy (14:21). Often, people search for logical explanations as to why these specific rules came about. Why these rules and not others? Is it good for human health to keep kosher? Is it about self-control? Is it something else entirely? Regardless, *kashrut* is known as a *mitzvah* you do even if you do not understand the complete reasoning behind it.

Kashrut means "to separate" specific foods from one another (meat and dairy). It also means there are foods you do not eat at all—no shellfish, including shrimp and clams, or pork products. We eat only fish with both scales and fins. For example, salmon and halibut are perfect choices. Animals we eat must have split hooves and chew their cud. Chicken, cow, and duck are all acceptable, but pork is no good. Mixing of milk with meat products is not permitted (a cheeseburger or pepperoni pizza is a no-no), and it is required that you wait between eating meat and having cheesecake for dessert, as dairy cannot follow soon after a meat meal. How long you must wait between meat and dairy depends on your family's tradition or your rabbi's advice. Buying meat that is kosher-supervised is preferable, as Judaism has special rules about slaughtering animals for eating. You can find kosher meat markets in many states. Online ordering makes it even easier! And, of course, if you climbed this high on the *kashrut* ladder, then you know that many people keep separate dishes and utensils for dairy meals and for meat meals.

It is interesting to note that the root for *kashrut*—*kaf, shin,* and *reish* (כ.ש.ר)—is the same as the word for "weight room," *chadar kosher,* where one goes to get fit. In other words, keeping kosher is what is fitting for us to eat.

I remember when my daughter was a freshman in college, and her friends wanted to celebrate with her the "real" freedom from her parents by taking her to a non-kosher restaurant. My daughter was bewildered by this and responded that *she* is keeping kosher because *she* wants to keep it, not because someone is forcing her. Our household operates on love and understanding. My husband and I have never perceived the *kashrut* laws as restrictive and prohibitive. We look at the laws not only as choices and privileges, but also as a way to connect to God by following the commandments. I *get* to keep kosher. I *do* remember who I am every time I eat. I *am* a Jewish person who acts Jewishly every day and every meal. How lucky am I?!

Your Personal Lev Moment

1. Create a meal log for one week. You can do this in your iPhone Notes. Observe the results. Would you like to try keeping kosher? Begin by cutting out the clearly non-kosher food items (pork, shrimp, etc.). Do this until it is comfortable for you. If you wish to continue, separate your dairy and meat. Don't eat them together. Cheeseburgers and chicken Alfredo are out, dear reader! If you do this successfully, pat yourself on the back—you are almost keeping kosher! Start easy. Otherwise, kosher laws can become overwhelming, and you might quit before giving it a chance.

2. How do you think food intake elevates or changes who you are? When you plan your kosher meal, does the concept of Judaism enter your reasoning in choosing your food?

3. Have you ever considered that eating could be viewed as a religious act? Do you treat food and eating with a reverent outlook? Do you take time to prepare your meal, sit at a table, and enjoy the food you have prepared? Or are you distracted with other tasks and eat in the car on the way somewhere or in front of the TV while watching a show? If so, you might begin by making mealtime a special time of the day.

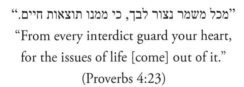

"מכל משמר נצור לבך, כי ממנו תוצאות חיים."
"From every interdict guard your heart,
for the issues of life [come] out of it."
(Proverbs 4:23)

Everyone Needs God's Help Sometimes

"אדוני שפתי תפתח ופי יגיד תהילתך."
"Adonai s'fatai tiftach ufi yagid tehilatechah."
"Oh Lord, You shall open my lips,
and my mouth will recite Your praise"
(Psalms 51:17).

J ews sing this verse before we begin the Amidah, the central prayer in every synagogue service that traditional Jews pray three times a day: morning, afternoon, and evening. Do you know the origin of this particular verse? Let's look at 2 Samuel 11–12 for more insight.

King David was looking out from his balcony and saw a beautiful woman on a nearby roof. Her name was Bat-Sheva. He decided to have her as his wife. But there was a problem. Bat-Sheva was married to a soldier name Uriah. King David arranged for her husband to be killed in battle by ordering Uriah to the frontline.

After her husband died, King David married Bat-Sheva and had a child with her. Sometime later, Nathan The Prophet approached the king and shared a story about a rich man who had many sheep but was interested in one poor man's sheep, which he forcefully took.

"That is horrible," King David exclaimed. "This man should be punished."

"That man is you," replied Nathan. It took Nathan's reproach for King David to realize his wrongdoing. King David was lost, not knowing how to right a wrong.

In Psalms, a book King David is credited with writing, he shares with us something that is universal: Sometimes we cannot bring ourselves to recognize and acknowledge our part in creating a situation in which we get entangled.

At times, we are all just like King David. Not that we have committed such a grave sin, but we have done things we should not have done. Regrettable actions and words put us in spiritual exile, exile from our friends and community, even exile from God. Perhaps, most importantly, we are in exile from our own better selves. We might feel helpless because we don't know how to approach God, how to do teshuvah (repentance), and how to return to our better self.

So we ask God. We plead, "God, open my lips so my mouth will speak your praise." The power of speech was given to us by God and is what differentiates us from animals. But we need help to learn how to use it. In Proverbs we read: ".מות וחיים ביד הלשון ואוהביה יאכל פריה"—"Death and life are in the hand of the tongue, and those who love it will eat its produce" (18:21). We can use our speech to kill or we can use our mouth to build and sustain. The power is in our hands, or should I say our tongues?

Your Personal Lev Moment

1. Try to say these six Hebrew words from Psalms 51:17 every morning as you start your day and every night before going to bed. Then add at least one statement of praise to God. I recall a phrase my parents use all the time when they want to express their praise of God. They speak these words when they hear good news in the family, or if a disaster was prevented. The phrase comes from Psalms 118:1 "Give thanks to the Lord because He is good, for His kindness is eternal."— *"Hodu l'Adonai ki tov, ki l'olam chasdo."*

2. Since you are asking God for help, explain to God why you need the help. Why does your mouth need to be opened? How does God help you bring about the words that come out?

3. There is so much about our speech that we are not aware of. In Judaism, there is a concept called *lashon harah*, which roughly translates as the "evil tongue." How aware are you of the words you utter? This week, reflect on your verbal and nonverbal communication: What messages do you send out to the universe? Would you change any of it?

"הנה עשיתי כדבריך הנה נתתי לך לב חכם ונבון
אשר כמוך לא היה לפניך ואחריך לא יקום כמוך."
"Behold, I have done according to your word;
behold, I have given you a wise and understanding
heart; so that there was none like you before you,
nor after you shall any arise like you."
(1 Kings 3:12)

Keep the Celebration Going

Birthdays—don't we all love them? The celebration, the congratulations, the love you receive, the fact you are just "one year" older than you were a day ago. It's a day all about you! We should rejoice and enjoy the day fully!

Can you guess the only birthday mentioned in the Torah? It was not Avraham's or Isaac's or even Jacob's. It was not a Hebrew's birthday. It was none other than the birthday of one of the Egyptian pharaohs! His birthday is mentioned when he arranges a feast for himself and decides what to do with the butler and the baker. Check out the story in Genesis 40.

This got me thinking. Which life cycle in Judaism has more importance associated with it, a birthday or the passing of a loved one? Both life cycles represent ends of the spectrum. In Judaism, there is much more emphasis given to someone's passing than their birth. Jews have the *Yizkor* (יזכור) prayer, a prayer we recite during a funeral and at every anniversary of the passing of a relative. Many people go to a synagogue on the anniversary of someone's death to remember them and recite this prayer. It is not that we do not remember their birthday, but their last day is the one we commemorate.

The question, of course, is why? Why do we go to synagogues to commemorate the passing of a family member rather than their birth? Why now?

To begin with, our birth has nothing to do with us; it is really the achievement of our parents. In a deeper sense, when we commemorate the passing of someone, it is an indication of how this person lived their life—their achievements and their influence and impact on us. What they leave behind is more than material items. What we are left with is their wisdom and the valuable lessons they taught us.

Your Personal Lev Moment

1. Can you connect choices you have made to the influence of a particular individual from your past? When you think of your family and the friends you have accumulated over the years, what have you learned from them that you want to keep and pass onto the next generation? What are three values you have instilled in your children and want them to carry forward long after you pass on?

2. What impact do you hope to make that will stay with your family for years to come? How do you want to be remembered? Can you write down five values and concepts you hope your family will carry forward?

3. I challenge you, on your next birthday, to call your parents and thank them, if they are still alive. You could even deliver flowers if you live close enough! There is great value in giving credit to the parent who did all the work to make your birthday a day worth celebrating. Your parent will feel

so special, and a gift is even better when it isn't given on an expected day like Mother's Day or Father's Day!

The day we were born is a joyful day for us and for our parents and families because we were brought into this world, into this existence. The time of our passing will show how impactful we were while in this world. That impact is determined by our cumulative actions, beginning today!

I wish for each and every one of us to live to the age of 120 and to celebrate each and every birthday, but always remember that what is most important is what we do the other 364 days of the year!

"לב שמח ייטב גהה ורוח נכאה תיבש–גרם."
"A happy heart enhances one's brilliance,
and a broken spirit dries the bones."
(Proverbs 17:22)

Loyalty vs. Freedom

I recently turned fifty! I think of the importance of the number "fifty" in Judaism and what it represents. The Jubilee year is biblically known as the year of freedom, the year in which slaves are set free and the land is returned to its original owners. How else does the number "fifty" symbolize freedom? On the fiftieth day after the Exodus from Egypt, the Jews received the Torah at Mount Sinai, and we became one people, the people of Israel, the Jewish nation. Receiving those laws turned us into a free nation. "Fifty" represents freedom.

As I have said before, letters in Hebrew have numerical equivalence. For example, *alef* equals one, *bet* equals two, *gimmel* equals three, and so on. The letter that represents the value of fifty is the letter *nun* (נ). The letter *nun* embodies the concept of servitude in the Hebrew language. The word for "loyalty" in Hebrew is *ne'eman* (נאמן), which has two *nuns,* one at the beginning and one at the end.

Perhaps this is because true servitude begins and ends with loyalty. Moses is known as *Eved Ne'eman* (עבד נאמן), or "a loyal servant." One of the greatest leaders in Jewish history is known as someone who loyally served God and the people of Israel. A leader who served something bigger than himself. Can you imagine a leader today calling themselves a "servant"?

As I celebrate the completion of my fifth decade, I call on my past experiences to lead me into freedom, all while being loyal to that which is bigger than me—to the almighty God who guides me and watches over me in ways I cannot describe. I pray God will continue to lead us to rely on our wisdom to achieve a positive balance between our personal sense of freedom and our calling to serve God with loyalty and dedication. To life! *L'chayim!*

Your Personal Lev Moment

1. Have you ever served the needs of others? How did this make you feel? Did you feel a sense of humility? Gratitude? Pride?
2. Can you think of one example where loyalty was the reason you did a service? How did it make you feel?
3. When you think of freedom, what synonyms come into your mind? How do you "live freedom" while still acknowledging your obligations as well as your rights?

"Man is never nearer the Divine
than in his compassionate moments."[3]
–Joseph H. Hertz

Chamber Four

RELATIONSHIP WITH ISRAEL AND JEWISH LIFE EVENTS

Glowing from the Inside Out

J ews are known as *or lagoyim* (אור לגויים)—"a light unto the
nations." What does this mean? How can we be a light unto
someone else? What makes you have a "glow" that affects another
person?

When Jewish people celebrate the holiday of Chanukah, we light
the *chanukiah*, also known as the *menorah*, and celebrate our liberation
from Greek control. Chanukah is a holiday that takes place in late
November or in December and commemorates the rededication of the
Holy Temple at the time of the Maccabean revolt in the year 168 BCE.
It is known as the "Holiday of Lights," or *Chag Ha-Urim*. In today's
world, many Jews have fun celebrating Chanukah by exchanging gifts,
making *latkes* (potato pancakes), and singing songs while playing
with a *dreidel*. Yet the holiday's history is crucial for the survival of
Jewish people. If it were not for the group of Jewish people who rose
up against the Greeks, Judaism would not be in existence today. They

ensured the survival of the Jewish people! This makes me contemplate the essence of our rights and our duties!

In American culture, we concern ourselves with our rights—freedom of speech, freedom of religion, freedom of assembly, etc. Judaism concerns itself with *mitzvot*, the Torah-based commandments requiring action. I think of responsibility and obligation. While freedom is of crucial importance and value to us, the emphasis in Judaism is on what we do for other people. To say it differently, Judaism focuses its essence not on what we receive, but on what we give and how we behave. How we conduct our lives and how we make others feel is of value in determining the kind of person we are.

Here is a little Hebrew gem—the Hebrew word for "right" (as in "the right to something") is *zechut*, which comes from the root *zayin*, *chaf*, and *hey* (ז.כ.ה), the same as for the word that means "win." This word *zechut* is not mentioned in the Torah. Interestingly, there are two words that mean "to win" in Hebrew: *lenatzeach* (לנצח) and *lizkot* (לזכות). What's the difference? *Lenatzeach* is to win in a competition or a war. It involves defeating others and achieving victory over someone else. *Lizkot* is a word you use when you receive something as a reward, not necessarily in a competitive way, but because you earned or deserved it.

So when do we truly win? When we beat others to it? No, true winning and reward does not come from meaningless competition, but when we take action to deserve it.

Your Personal Lev Moment

1. Try to find an opportunity each day to carry out an act of kindness for someone else. Visit the sick, offer to help carry groceries for someone, cook for a family in need, or offer up your seat on a crowded bus when you see a person who would benefit more from sitting.

2. Be a light unto another person at least once this week. Support them in their endeavors, in their efforts. Observe how this makes you feel. Record your experience and observation in your journal.

3. Do you have a competitive nature? If so, can you focus your energy and attention this week on receiving a reward and not necessarily a prize for winning? Do you feel the difference within you? Do you feel the difference in how you make others feel?

On Being Thankful and Jewish

The word *Jew* in Hebrew is *Yehudi* (*Yehudia* for a female). Since the Hebrew language is root-based, you now know almost every word in the Hebrew language is built from three letters known as "consonants." As a reminder, the three consonants not only form that particular word, but are the base for other words as well (which sometimes connects two separate words—a completely foreign concept in the English language). The root of the word *Jew* (יהודי) is also the same as the word that means "to be thankful." Leah, one of the Jewish matriarchs married to Jacob, named her fourth son Judah for this reason—she was thankful to God for giving her this son.

Moreover, the first prayer a Jew utters as they wake in the morning is the *Modeh Ani*; we thank God for giving us our soul and consciousness back after a night's rest (*The Complete Artscroll Siddur*, p. 2). The first two words are of critical importance. *Modeh Ani* literally translates as "Thank I" rather than what you would expect to be proper grammatical order, "I thank." Isn't this odd? Shouldn't these two words be in reverse order? Usually in Hebrew, as well as in English, the subject of a sentence comes before the verb. So, logically, you would expect it to read as "I thank." But not in this prayer! Why?

When we open our eyes first thing in the morning, before we even step one foot out of bed, our first thoughts should be of gratitude. We are invited to put the subject of the sentence—I—only secondarily. How often are we really and truly grateful? This prayer teaches us to be thankful and reminds us to think selflessly, with "I" coming second to gratitude.

Here is your chance. Just as the holiday of Thanksgiving is a reminder to be thankful, let us invite gratitude into our daily practice. It is interesting to note that the Pilgrims took the idea of thankfulness from the holiday of Sukkot, known as the "Festival of Booths," mentioned in the Bible. What we say becomes a reflection of who we are and what we value. Many Jews start their morning giving thanks, increasing our ability to be thankful throughout the day. Judaism teaches us to be grateful by incorporating prayers such as this one into our morning routine. I invite each and everyone one of us to be thankful for all we have and who we are. It does us good.

Your Personal Lev Moment

1. Avoid complaining for one day! If this is easy for you, try for one week. Grab your journal and record your thoughts. How did you feel?

2. Say "thank you" every morning when you wake up. Say it aloud and state specifically why you are thankful. Is it because your back does not hurt? Is it because you have a job? Is it because you are able to provide for your family? Is it because you are alive? All these reasons are worthy—verbalize them.

3. Start a week by thanking one person in your life on the first day, then gradually increase to two people on the third day, and three people on the fifth day. Write down in your journal the reason you are thankful for them. Did they smile when they saw you? Did they help you in any way? Did they do what you asked them? Pay attention to all the details.

4. Observe how your gratitude influences your recipients. Don't be surprised if they take your lead and thank others. Before you know it, you will start a gratitude movement.

5. Notice how the benefits of kindness that you show to others slowly improves your sleeping patterns, your feelings of self-worth, and your health (your heart as well as your immune system).

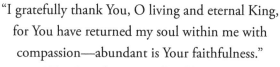

"מודה אני לפניך מלך חי וקיים שהחזרת
בי נשמתי בחמלה רבה אמונתך."

"I gratefully thank You, O living and eternal King,
for You have returned my soul within me with
compassion—abundant is Your faithfulness."
(*The Complete Artscroll Siddur*, p. 2)

If I Forget Thee, Jerusalem

My wedding—I remember the day as if it were yesterday, when, in actuality, it was over thirty years ago.

I met my husband in 1984. I was just eighteen years old and about to join the Israeli military, and Bob was a young twenty-three-year-old American visiting his religious school teacher who had made *aliyah* (immigration to Israel) some years prior. At the time, I was in a program that exposed city kids to *kibbutz* life. *Kibbutz* comes from the Hebrew word *kevutzah*, meaning "group of individuals." A *kibbutz* is a place unique to Israel created by a group of people who share the vision of a socialist community in which Jewish people live in a communal framework. They share economic resources and work together as a team to build a better life for all. They work the land together, they share meals, and they share their profits.

That is where Bob and I met. He volunteered to work in the apple fields where I had been assigned to pick apples during the autumn

season. Coincidence? I see it as fate! Fast forward four years: Bob had
returned to Israel three more times. During his fourth visit, we were
under the wedding canopy, bonded in marriage for life.

There are many rituals at a Jewish wedding. I would like to
concentrate on one verse a groom is required to say shortly before
breaking the glass with his foot: "If I forget thee, O Jerusalem, may
my right hand wither" (Psalms 137:5). What does Jerusalem have to
do with a wedding? Why do we need to remember this particular city?
While the breaking of the glass is a symbolic act of mourning for the
destruction of the Temple and the Jews' expulsion from the land of
Israel into Babylon, for me, it is much more.

This ritual is a reminder of what Israel represents for Jews all
over the world—the yearning to have our own land, our own state,
a place we can call a homeland. This ritual is the connection of every
Jew, secular or religious, to a place we can all call home. Israel is a
place where Jewish history comes alive, where every stone has a story
connected to the Bible and to our collective history. To remember
Jerusalem in our joyous moment, in the moment when we declare
loyalty to one another, is significant. Not only do we declare our
faithfulness to our partner with whom we are planning to spend the
rest of our lives, but we also declare loyalty to the land and to the
vision of a Jewish homeland for the Jewish people.

Over the years, as Bob and I built our lives together and raised our
children, we shared our love and connection to Israel with our family.
We visited the land; we learned its songs. We tasted from its food,
and we met its people. We followed Israel on the daily news, and we
prayed for its safety. We cried with the people, and we surely celebrated
their victories as well. At the time I am writing this book, Israel is
celebrating seventy years of existence as a recognized country. In a
region that has suffered so much turbulence, the reality that Israel is on
the world map is miraculous.

Jews pray daily facing east, toward Jerusalem. We pray for peace in Jerusalem. In our daily prayer we say, "May the One who creates peace in the heavens bring peace among us and all of Israel and let us say, Amen." And may it be so!

Your Personal Lev Moment

1. What do you know about Israel? This week, discover three new facts about the land of Israel and its miraculous existence.

2. Have you visited Israel? Make an effort this week to meet an Israeli and talk to them about their homeland. Or visit www.ynet.com for the latest news about Israel.

3. Have you exposed yourself to Israeli staple food? Try falafel and hummus this week in a Middle Eastern restaurant.

4. Have you listened to Israeli music? Go on YouTube or any other music channel to find the recent hits in Israel. It may take time for you to develop a taste for this music, but give it a chance—it is beautiful!

5. Israel is a leading country in technological innovations. Surprise yourself and research Israeli inventions. How many items invented in Israel do you, your family, and your friends use daily?

Dorice and her husband, Bob, on their wedding in Israel, February 1988

”אם אשכחך ירושלים תשכח ימיני, תדבק לשוני לחיכי אם
לא אזכרכי אם לא אעלה את ירושלים על ראש שמחתי.“

"If I forget you, O Jerusalem, may my right
hand forget [its skill]. May my tongue cling to
my palate, if I do not remember you, if I do not
bring up Jerusalem at the beginning of my joy."
(Psalms 137:5–6)

Time to Say Goodbye

Baruch Dayan Emet (ברוך דיין אמת)—"The Blessed and True Judge" is the phrase Jews are invited to say upon hearing of someone's passing (Talmud, *Brachot* 9b). These words recognize God as the true Judge who knows the time span each individual has lived on this earth. All of what God does shows truth. At the time when we are most in grief, we place the responsibility on our God for what has been taken away from us.

My friend lost her father recently. This loss brought up many memories from when my husband's parents passed away, almost a decade ago. How do you move on? Can you move on? What do you do as a mourner? Can Judaism shed light, and maybe a bit of hope, when life is dark and sad?

My friend's dad passed away at the ripe old age of ninety-four. We received the call on a Thursday morning, and the immediate question we asked was "What can we do to help?" My friend asked me to join her at the synagogue to organize our thoughts so we knew what to ask the rabbi. In times of grief, a person is often worried. We wanted to make sure we covered all the bases. I drove her to the funeral home to sort out payments and to help remember the details to relate later to the family. I made it a priority to encourage her to eat so that she could sustain herself through the day. I was worried she might collapse.

Once it was determined the burial would take place on Sunday, I shifted my thinking to consider sustenance for the entire family—twenty-six people were gathering together on Friday night for a traditional Sabbath meal. After discussing my emerging idea with my husband and my fifteen-year-old son, we offered ourselves as the chefs and servers for the meal. I arrived home on Thursday evening and prepared my traditional sweet and sour meatballs, my Persian rice, potato-filled pastries called *burekas*, and chicken soup. Another friend made salad and roasted vegetables, and we were set!

My husband, Bob, my son Yaniv, and I arrived at their house on Friday evening at 6:00, and we stayed in the kitchen for the majority of the evening. We served the food, we cleaned off the tables, we washed the dishes, and we put them away. We left when we finished all the dishes and swept the kitchen. There are not enough words in any language to describe the degree of gratitude our friends conveyed. In the midst of their great sorrow, they saw what life was all about—being there for one another, helping in time of need.

The statement we say when we hear of the passing of a dear one is very telling. The word *emet*, or "truth," is built from three special letters: the first letter of the Hebrew alphabet (א), the middle letter (מ), and the very last letter of the Hebrew alphabet (ת). The word *emet* spans over all the letters of the alphabet, from beginning to end and through the middle. A life of truth is ultimately what we want to strive toward, starting at the very beginning of our life and all the way through to the end. We may look at *emet* as the entire span of our existence, with the hope that we lead a life infused with truth.

I overheard my friend's family recalling stories which made their father's life be an example to all their future descendants. He lived a life full of truth. I realized that the way to move on is to take the time, as painful as the loss may feel, to relive the past. To honor the past and the contribution of the deceased in their present life is a healthy process. This is what Judaism allows and encourages. I witnessed the value of giving without the expectation of receiving. I experienced the exhilarating sensation of showing kindness and wanting to do a *mitzvah* (a commandment or, as many will substitute, "a good deed") for someone who was suffering.

Here are my friend's beautiful words of appreciation, so you, too, can feel inspired to do your own good for someone in need:

"Dorice - I can't express what you and Bob and Yaniv did for our family tonight. *HaShem* [God] sends people into your lives for a reason. As you say, *mishpuchah* [the term we use when our friends behave like family] friends are there for all the *simchas* together. But to be there for you in times of sadness or other needs, that is something else. You have carried me along these last two days like a battery pack at my side. I'm not sure how I would have got through it without you. As I said to you, *'ein milim'* [there are no words]. I love you so much. You are a true friend and performed a huge *mitzvah* this week. I wish you a long life and for your light to forever shine."

Your Personal Lev Moment

1. Have you ever experienced the loss of a loved one? Who was it? How long ago? How did you mourn?
2. Have you ever been on the giving end when a friend suffered a loss? In what ways have you shown your support and love? How did you help? What are your memories of this time?

3. Can you think of one example of a *mitzvah* you did which made a significant impact on others? How did this make you feel?

A Forever Promise

I f there is one moment in a person's life that shakes them and changes their course, it is most certainly having children, by birth or adoption. From the moment a human being becomes a parent, their life is forever changed. Overnight, a new title is added to the person's identity. Now they are a parent. They become fully responsible for another human being's existence. What a task! What a magnificent responsibility! What a privilege! I was gifted this merit to become a parent to three fantastic individuals, each different than the other, each with their own style, strengths, character, and wishes. I remember their arrivals in this world as if it were yesterday. I am sure many of you who read this can relate.

When a Jewish child is born, according to Jewish tradition, boys have a circumcision ceremony on the eighth day after their birth. This follows the story in Genesis where "God said to Abraham, 'And as for you, you shall keep My covenant [*brit*], you and your offspring after you, throughout their generations. This is My covenant which you shall keep, between Me and you and your offspring after you. Every male among you shall be circumcised. You shall circumcise the flesh of your foreskin, and that shall be the sign of the covenant between Me and you" (Genesis 17:9–11).

The word *circumcision* in Hebrew is built from two words—*Brit Milah*. The first word *brit* (ברית) appears often in the Torah, no fewer than 200 times. For example, in Genesis, God tells Noah, "ואני הנני מקים את בריתי אתכם ואת זרעכם אחריכם."—"And as for Me, behold, I establish My covenant with you and your offspring after you" (9:9). God also instructs Avraham regarding Isaac, "והקימותי את בריתי איתו לברית עולם."—"And I will fulfill My covenant with him as an everlasting covenant for his offspring after him" (Genesis 17:19). Here, the word we use for *brit* is translated as "covenant." A quick internet search for the definition of *covenant* yields agreement, promise, contract.

What I find fascinating in this Jewish ritual is that a person (the parent) is entering a contract with God regarding another completely different human (the child). From the moment our baby is born, a Jewish parent promises to raise them in a certain way, with a certain identity and heritage. When else in life do we promise something like this? Under what circumstances do we take responsibility for the future affiliations of our children?

This view of circumcision ritual makes this entry suitable for several of the chambers within this book because it represents the different relationships we foster during our lifetime. It can beautifully fit in Chamber Two, highlighting the relationships we have with other people and how we transfer the love of Judaism to them. This entry also belongs in Chamber Three, as part of our relationship to God. Moreover, this entry can obviously be included in Chamber Four,

Jewish Life Events, and its implication is a once-in-a-lifetime event that changes who you are.

Despite a small number of Jews who have chosen not to circumcise their children, circumcision is as popular today as it was generations ago. With all the development and modernization of society and the letting go of whatever seems to be "archaic," *Brit Milah* has not become a thing of the past. Jews all over the world, in all streams of Judaism, advocate for this ritual. We want to ask ourselves why. Why do I need to participate in this "old tradition"? While for more traditional Jews, this ceremony is a commandment from the Torah and therefore is sufficient reason to continue it without questioning, I think for many others, the answer lies in what I have unfolded above— that we take responsibility for the collective future of those who cannot yet promise. We, as adults, know the treasures of our tradition, so we are committed to transfer them to the next generation.

What about the birth of girls? Even though a ritual called *zeved habat*, meaning "the gift of a girl," has been practiced for many generations, in recent years, the beautiful tradition known as *simchat habat*—"the rejoicing of a girl"—has surfaced as a modern and progressive Jewish ritual. These celebrations can include women singing psalms and dancing or a father called up to the Torah during services to welcome the new addition to the family. These meaningful customs provide an egalitarian perspective, giving equal importance to both genders. When our daughter was born, my husband and I invited over one hundred people to his parents' backyard for a *simchat habat* celebration. We served cookies and refreshments, we bestowed blessings on our daughter, and people welcomed her into our community with song and dance. It was as joyous an event as the *Brit Milah* ceremonies our boys had.

When God gave the Torah to the Israelites in the desert, they responded with "*Na'aseh v'nishma.*" ("נעשה ונשמע.")—"We will do, and we will obey" (Exodus 24:7). The promise of old is still true today as we give our promise to God to follow His commandments for the unforeseen future by teaching the essence of Judaism to our children. Our rich heritage gives us the ability to transfer a meaningful inheritance to our future. Belonging to the "Jewish Tribe" may be a treasure for today's Jews, but it is also an incredible responsibility for future generations.

Your Personal Lev Moment

1. Have you attended a circumcision ceremony or a *zeved habat*? What was a ritual or an aspect you appreciated?
2. How do you process the fact that promises are made on behalf of the entire Jewish people to God?
3. How does a collective responsibility, or *achrayut meshutefet* (אחריות משותפת), for the future mesh with your life values?
4. Have you ever made a promise that was ultimately not dependent on you? If so, how did you follow up on the promise? How involved were you in making sure the promise was fulfilled?

"Therefore, every person must say,
'For my sake, the world was created.'"
(Talmud, *Mishnah Sanhedrin* 4:5)

Special Lev Moment Introduction

O ur hearts fill with joy when we celebrate special moments in life. In the following pages, you will read treasured *Lev Moments* that do just that—fill us up with wisdom and joy as we transition from one life stage to another. I spent sixteen years of my professional life as the Director of Education in a conservative synagogue in Portland, Oregon. During this time, I was honored to have the privilege and the gift of opportunity to share with congregants their life cycle events, from *Brit Milah* ceremonies to B'nai Mitzvah to weddings and, yes, even funerals. The entries that follow are but a small glimpse into that fantastic aspect of some of my personal highlights—words I have spoken at several B'nai Mitzvah ceremonies, graduations, and a wedding.

If you are an educator, a parent, a guardian, or just someone who cares, you are welcome to use the following entries as inspiration for your teaching and transferring the light of Judaism in your own environment. While some are more personal than others, all of them have a message by which to live. You are welcome to glean wisdom from them for your own purposes, even if only to read to your child. I hope you will find just the right one to share with your loved ones, allowing the light in this world and in this book to reach as far as it possibly can.

In the following pages are words from my heart, and I sincerely hope they enter yours. As you read these special *Lev Moments* (*Moments of the Heart*), I invite you to think of similar moments in your life and the lives of the precious people around you.

"מכל מלמדי השכלתי ומתלמידי יותר מכולם."
"I have learned much from my teachers
and most from my students."
(*Ta'anit* 7a)

Secrets to Success
For High School Graduates

Here we are at the end of one road and the beginning of a beautiful, yet perhaps slightly scary, path ahead—scary because what lies ahead is unknown and untraveled. Speaking for myself, sometimes the unknown can be scary: new experiences, new people, new learning. Finding our way can be challenging and, more importantly, unnerving because life tests us through the way we behave when we face these challenges.

How meaningful it is to celebrate school graduation around the same time as the holiday of Shavuot, when the Jewish people received both the oral and written Torah, which includes the Ten Commandments—the blueprint of ethical living and thinking. It would only be fitting for me to give you a few extra insights from our tradition (or you could call them commandments). I hope you will find them useful at this particular junction of your life as you leave the house you know as your *bayit* (home).

"נכנס יין יצא סוד. "

"Nichnas yayin yatza sod."

"Wine enters and a secret exits" (Talmud, *Masechet Sanhedrin* 38a).

Too many times we have all seen what intoxicating substances can do. They are very powerful. (And may I say that not everything that is legal is good.) Be careful not to change that which you love about yourself because others do or because you can. Judge and decide for yourself what kind of person you really want to be.

"אל תסתכל בקנקן אלא במה שיש בו. "

"Al tistakeil bakankan ela bemah sheyeish bo."

"Don't judge a vessel by its outside appearance, but look inside" (*Pirkei Avot* 4:27).

There is a story about a king who advertised a competition to determine who in his kingdom could find the best wine for him. People went into a frenzy as they searched the country to find the best winery. One man found the most amazing winery with the most delicious wine. He decided to put the wine in a golden vessel, as is fitting for a king. He packaged the golden vessel and carried it on a donkey's back to the palace. When the man brought the wine to the king, he poured it into a golden cup and handed it to the king. The king tasted the wine, but spit it out of his mouth in disgust. The wine had spoiled because of the way it was stored—a golden vessel is not the best way to keep wine.

What can we learn from this? Sometimes people might seem important because of their title, status, or wealth, but they are not really who they appear to be or as important as you might think. Their "golden vessel" doesn't mean their insides are "golden." In other words, their outside appearance is not a true reflection of who they are. Get to know people for who they are on the inside.

"אל תאמר לכשאפנה אשנה שמא לא תפנה."

"Al tomar k'she'efneh eshneh shema lo tifneh."

"And do not say, 'When I am free I will study' for perhaps you will not become free" (*Pirkei Avot* 2:5).

Don't procrastinate. Don't let life happen to you. Be the movers and the shakers. Plan ahead; be prepared!

"מודה אני לפניך."

"Modeh ani l'fanecha."

"Gratefully thank I You" (This is the exact order.) (*The Complete Artscroll Siddur*, p. 2).

Have and show gratitude. There will be times in your life when you will be with people who might not be grateful or demonstrate gratitude. Be the light; be the leader. Model how different behavior can have different results. Show others how thankfulness and appreciation come first. Set the tone for you and for others around you.

"קנה לך חבר."

"Kneih lechah chaveir."

"Buy yourself a friend" (*Pirkei Avot* 1:6).

The ancient rabbis didn't mean for us to buy friends with money, but with generosity—generosity of actions, generosity of deeds, generosity of thoughts, and generosity of speech.

To all the graduates: *derech tzlachah* (דרך צלחה) —may you have an enriching and successful road ahead.

Your Personal Lev Moment

1. Have you ever consumed alcohol to the point of regret? Why? What needed to happen for you to realize that you might want to seek a different way to express yourself? How did you change your ways?
2. In what ways do you show generosity toward your friends?

3. Have you ever judged someone by their appearance and were disappointed or surprisingly pleased? Why?

4. How do you gain friends? Think of the longest friendships you have maintained so far. Do they have anything in common that contribute to their longevity?

Contemporary Habits
Meet Ancient Wisdom
For High School Graduates

I am sure your parents can give you plenty of advice and thoughtful parting words as you move onto the next exciting phase in your life, but allow me to tell you a story. Once upon a time, a girl was born to the most wonderful parents. She was the first-born child and the only daughter, and her parents were so thrilled about the opportunities that would present themselves to their girl. So, for eighteen years, they strove to love her unconditionally and to teach her morals and lessons necessary for a sound foundation. They surrounded her with friends and family, school, and synagogue.

And then, this girl met me. I gave her the following advice about social media:

Facebook: The world has a chance to see everything you post or comment. Isn't it interesting that the word *face* in English comes from the Greek word meaning "a mask," while in Hebrew the word is *panim*, which shares the same root as the Hebrew word *bifnim*, meaning "inside." If you can relate to this connection between "face" and "inside," you value face-to-face interactions because you can see what is truly on the inside of a person. When you post something on Facebook, keep in mind that most people present a "mask" on their Facebook wall. Be careful what you show the world. Make sure people can see the real light inside of you, a light that shines.

Twitter: Birds tweet, and the more they tweet, the louder the sound becomes. Somehow it seems that Twitter posts don't have the same weight and importance as if we spoke them aloud. Shimon, the son of Rabbi Gamliel, said in *Pirkei Avot*, "Throughout my life I was raised among scholars, and I discovered that nothing becomes a person more than silence" (1:17). Sometimes not responding is the right thing to do. Measure your words—once you post, you cannot take them back.

Instagram: Nothing satisfying in this life is truly instant. Believe no one who tells you differently. Anything worthwhile takes effort, dedication, hard work, sweat, and time. Our goals are all achievable with this mindset. As I was growing up, my mother would quote a verse from Genesis every time she wanted me to work hard to achieve something worth achieving: *"Bezei'at apechah tochal lechem."* ("בזעת אפיך תאכל לחם.")—"By the sweat of your brow you shall eat bread" (3:19).

Snapchat: I think of immediate gratification when I think of Snapchat, as if someone snaps their fingers and reality becomes a fact. Snapping your fingers is not the automatic (or polite) signal for beginning a conversation. Yes, it is nice to share with the world what is going on in a moment, but be careful not to use this social media platform as the main way to share what is going on in your life. Your life is so much richer and better than a Snapchat!

Our tradition offers wisdom and insights as to how to live your best life. Here are a few gems for you to take with you on your road of discovery!

I love the Hebrew word *achrayut* (אחריות), which means "responsibility," because the first three letters create another word. The word is *acher* (אחר), meaning "another." What does it mean to be responsible? If you look at this word through the Hebrew language lens, it means to be accountable to another person. One true meaning of responsibility is thinking about other people. Now is the time for you to be accountable not only to yourself, but also to the world around you. In order to do this well, you need to take care of yourself: get enough sleep, eat the right kinds of food, and drink lots of water. But don't forget that you are part of a community. Do not forget that once you take care of yourself, also take care of those around you. You are needed.

"למנות ימינו כן הודע ונביא לבב חוכמה."

"Limnot yameinu kein hodah v'navee levav chochmah."

"So teach the number of our days, so that we shall acquire a heart of wisdom" (Psalms 90:12).

Live every day with the acknowledgment and sense that you have been gifted a day. With each passing day, learn something new!

"עץ חיים היא למחזיקים בה ותומכיה מאושר."

"Eitz Chayim hee lamachazikim bah v'tomchehah me'ooshar."

"It is a Tree of Life for those who grasp it; those who draw near it are fortunate" (Proverbs 3:18).

Life boils down to living the ways of the Torah, of bringing the values of Torah into our daily life. Don't forsake who you are and where you came from. Remember that the Torah and, by extension, your community, are available to help, support, and celebrate with you. Be the best person you can be. This will give us much *nachat*—pride!

Your Personal Lev Moment

1. Take a week and do one small act of kindness for someone else. Count the days and count the deeds. Make the deeds reflect your days.

2. Do you take care of yourself? Too little? Too much? Do you also take care of others? How do you do this?

3. Do you believe in something/someone greater than you? What does this belief do to your understanding of the world and everything that happens in it?

4. Are you a social media user? What do you think are the dangers hidden in constant usage of these platforms? How can you balance the advantages and the disadvantages?

5. Have you witnessed cyberbullying or other inappropriate behavior online? What have you done to remedy this?

Choosing Goodness

You have accomplished your goals. Doesn't it feel so good? "Good," or *tov*, is a concept that appears in the first chapter of Genesis as God creates the world. He said, *"Ki tov"*—"and it was good." Today I would say you have done *tov meod*, very well!

Cultivating goodness is no easy task. Every person is born with the potential to do good. That quality is embodied in each one of us. We must, however, work on this quality daily, so it becomes a habit we are proud of. An adult reaching the goal of Bar Mitzvah is a living example of what it means to cultivate goodness. Every time you studied for this day, you demonstrated your goodness, your modesty, your humility, and your thirst to learn and grow as a person.

When God decided to create a partner for Adam, *"HaShem* God said, 'It is not good that man be alone; I will make him a helper corresponding to him.'"—*"Lo tov heyot haadam levado"* ("לא טוב היות האדם לבדו") (Genesis 2:18).

The topic of goodness is not only mentioned in the story of Genesis, but throughout the Torah, we have several examples of and directives for what is good and how to choose it.

"ראה נתתי לפניך היום את החיים ואת הטוב ואת המוות ואת הרע." In Deuteronomy, God tells the people: "See. I have placed before you today the life and the good, and the death and the evil" (30:15). While we can have a discussion on the topic of good vs. bad, I would like us to focus on the concept of choosing. Each one of us has the ability to choose how we live in this world, how we want to leave our stamp on the people (our family, our colleagues, our friends) we encounter every single day.

Each morning we awake, and the first words traditional Jews utter upon opening our eyes is a very short prayer that starts with the words: *"Modeh ani lefanechah"*—"Thank I You, oh God." What a fantastic way to exercise gratitude by saying the words "Thank You" upon rising. As we go to bed, a second before we fall asleep, we have yet another opportunity to exercise goodness. We whisper a special prayer called the *Shema al Hamita,* which means "the *Shema* on the bed."

"Master of the universe, I hereby forgive anyone who angered or antagonized me, or who has sinned against me…May it be Your will, *HaShem*, my God, and the God of my forefathers that I may sin no more…May the expression of my mouth and the thoughts of my heart find favor before You, *HaShem*, my Rock and my Redeemer" (*The Complete Artscroll Siddur*, p. 289).

Each one of us can choose gratitude, forgiveness, and goodness. We have the ability to choose. Let's celebrate this ability—choosing to be good, choosing to be grateful, and choosing to be happy. Choose to be a proud Jew. Choose to be a terrific human being!

Your Personal Lev Moment

1. Think of an action you regularly do to cultivate goodness. How does it make you feel? Do you need a partner to complete this action?

2. Can you come up with one new action each week? Make notes in your journal about these newly acquired actions.

3. Do you harbor negative feelings and struggle to let them go? If so, can you recite the *Shema* before going to bed? Google or YouTube its melody. Try singing it each night for a week. How does saying this prayer aloud make you feel? Does it in any way connect you to a higher purpose? Do you sleep better?

May these words, actions, and inspirations open new opportunities for you. May each one of you go from strength to strength—*Mechayil lechayil!*

You Shall Be Holy
Bar/Bat Mitzvah

The Torah portion *Kedoshim* has one of the most intriguing verses:
"והייתם קדשים כי קדוש אני ה' אלוהיכם."

God is telling us "You shall be holy, for holy am I, *HaShem* your God" (Leviticus 19:2).

I have been thinking about the concept of holiness for quite some time. Why do you think we should be holy? Should we strive for holiness just because God is holy? What is really the definition of being holy? Moreover, if God is like a parent or teacher to us, then maybe we could look at this from a parenting or teaching perspective.

As a parent, I know I have said to my own children more than once, "I want you to be (fill in the blank) because I am *this*." In our case, the word "this" can be a leader, someone who is generous, loves

Israel, or is devoted to Judaism. You can come up with your own words for "this."

As a teacher, I wish to share with my students the knowledge of the treasures that Judaism offers because I find them precious. I view Judaism, God, and the land of Israel as a privileged connection for the Jewish people. Many of us engage in pursuing various ethical discussions or social-action outings to learn something particular about our relationship to one another and to God. However, in the verse above, God is telling us something that is not specific. He is asking us to be holy. Therefore, I would suggest we look at the word *holy* as our "elevated self"—a self who keeps on improving as the years pass, but only as long as we keep working on ourselves!

A Bar Mitzvah marks a memorable day—a day when you are invited to be holy. Being holy does not just happen overnight, of course. For many years, you have put effort into learning, into understanding, and into being part of the community. Through all your preparation, the world around you saw a self-reflective young adult, a kind person, and a gentle soul. What we see when we look at you is sincerity and gentility. We see your sense of wonder of this world. May you continue to explore the holiness that is in you!

The concept of holiness is complex. I invite you to continue to study, search, and strive to discover the paths and avenues for holiness even if you don't know exactly what it means.

Your Personal Lev Moment

1. Do you have someone in your life whom you regard as holy? Who? Why do you perceive them as holy?
2. Do you believe you have holiness in you? How does this holiness manifest itself? What actions/thoughts do you experience that bring to light this belief?

3. If you were to cultivate holiness, what would be the first three things you would engage in? Can you start this week?

Author's son Matan graduating from college, May 2017

Hearing and Acting on It
Bar/Bat Mitzvah

You have reached the day your family has been looking forward to for so many years. I see before me a young adult who is caring, smart, and inquisitive—someone who wants to learn and wants to live life the best you can. In my teaching, I have seen a caring friend, a capable learner, and an ethical person!

The Torah portion *Shoftim* discusses judges and judging. There is a verse from this on which I always reflect.

"והגד־לך ושמעת ודרשת היטב והנה אמת נכון הדבר".

"And it will be told to you and you will hear; then you shall investigate well, and behold! It is true, the testimony is correct" (Deuteronomy 17:4).

Observe the level of introspection and care regarding how to handle what we hear. How fitting these words are every day of our

lives, but even more so before we enter the period of the
High Holy Days.

We hear numerous statements from friends, teachers, colleagues,
family, and the media. Do you simply take what you hear for granted,
or do you try to find what lies underneath these statements? How
do you sift through what you hear? How do you make your own
judgments regarding the truth? Our Torah gives us the tools for not
only introspection of our own lives, but also of the world around us.
Three verbs are used in this verse to truly verify what we hear. We are
told something, we *hear* it, and then we deeply *investigate* the truth to
see if the statement is indeed correct. We are directed not to take words
other people say for granted, but we must learn about their accuracy!

I wish for you a life of seeking the truth (*emet*). And once you
have it, hold on tight to it. There is a beautiful part at the end of the
Torah service, after the Torah is read and placed back into the ark—a
moment where all the congregants are standing, the curtain is open,
and all the community sings together: "It is a Tree of Life to those who
hold fast to it and all of its supporters are happy" (Proverb 3:18). The
Torah is our law, the Torah of truth. Go forth and spread this truth to
the world around you.

Your Personal Lev Moment

1. Have there been times in your life when you heard something
   about which you were very upset? What did you do? How did
   you verify the truth of it?
2. Think of a time when you heard something that caused you to
   look further into the matter? How did you do this? Did your
   investigation involve others? What was the outcome?

To the Groom on His Upcoming Wedding

We could not have been happier when our daughter, Hadas, told us she would love to marry you! When you were in dentistry school, you met her at a gelato shop while she was studying for her nursing degree. Just seven short weeks later, the two of you flew to meet us. For an entire week, we sat and talked about life. We discussed your hopes and visions for the future. We knew then that Hadas and you were meant to be with one another.

Our Jewish tradition tells us in the Talmud, *Tractate Eruvin* 65b, that a man is measured by three attributes: *kiso, koso, v'ka'aso* (כיסו, כוסו, וכעסו) his pocket, his cup, and his anger. What does this mean? What can we take from this ancient writing and apply to today's world?

Here is how I interpret this tradition as it connects to you on three levels. On the first level is how you relate to your fellow people, such as your young bride, your friends, and your colleagues. This is the *kiso* aspect. How generous are you, David, to our daughter and to those who surround you? "His pocket" (*kiso*): You have demonstrated generosity through the kind acts you have shown our daughter, our family, and all who surround you.

The second level is "his cup" (*koso*), which expresses how you relate to yourself. This is the rabbi's way of asking whether a person drinks a lot. If the answer is yes, this is not good. The relationship with the self is lacking. Someone who drinks heavily is more tempted by addiction and is someone who doesn't take care of themselves, which is not a favorable judgment. But you have proven that, while you love to have fun and connect with people, you are not dependent on any external influences. This is the way you are, and we love you for this admirable characteristic.

"His anger" (*ka'aso*) is the third level of relationship with the world. This is your connection to something outside of yourself, outside of the human being's control. I choose to call this "God." Are you someone who tends to see the world as a cup half full or half empty? Are you happy with your lot? Are you a grateful person? We are happy and blessed to hear and know that you rarely become angry. You and our daughter are a godly match, both complementing one another in the most beautiful way. My husband and I wish for you both a path full of love and understanding, a road rich in experiences, and a world full of goodness and success to enrich your lives forever.

Your Personal Lev Moment

1. *Kiso*, his pocket: How do you show your generosity? To whom? In what ways do you believe your generosity is connected to your relationship with others?

2. *Koso*, his drinking habits: Do you rely on external or unnatural substances to make you who you are? Do you let others define you, or do you define yourself by your own actions? Are you addicted to anything? How does that addiction affect you? In what ways do you reflect self-care and self-love? How does this love and care manifest itself in your everyday life?

3. *Ka'aso*, his anger: Are you quick to anger? Are you quick to calm down? How do you show your anger? Do you need to control your temper? If so, how do you do this?

4. Create a *kiso/koso/ka'aso* chart. Indicate instances when you showed who you really are in these three areas. Refer to the chart for a two-week period. Have at least three instances in each category that you can include on the chart. What brings your generosity to the surface? What triggers your anger, and how have you controlled it in this particular situation? When do you enjoy a glass of wine, and when is only one glass enough? Do you have difficulty controlling your impulses? Be aware of your behavior and evaluate if a change is needed.

David Mazor on his wedding day to Hadas Horenstein, author's daughter, August 2018

To the Bride on Her
Upcoming Wedding

A nyone who has watched *Fiddler on the Roof* probably remembers the words from the song "Matchmaker, Matchmaker" between sisters Chava and Hodel. Yes? Every bride, from the beginning of time, is yearning to find the perfect match.

"וַיֹּאמֶר ה' אֱלֹהִים לֹא־טוֹב הֱיוֹת הָאָדָם לְבַדּוֹ אֶעֱשֶׂה־לּוֹ עֵזֶר כְּנֶגְדּוֹ."

"Vayomer adonai elohim, lo tov heyot ha-adam levado, e-e-seh lo eizer k'negdo."

"*HaShem* said, 'It is not good that man is alone; I will make him a helper corresponding to him'" (Genesis 2:18).

What does it mean to be "a helpmate corresponding to him"? Is this a derogatory description? On the contrary—you, dear bride, have a task only you can do! Your contribution to the marriage is all in the spiritual realm. This is not to say you cannot work in a profession you love and contribute to the family finances, but your contribution to the marriage is far greater. The word *ezer*, which translates to "helper," shares the same root as the word *oz*, which means "spiritual strength." Without you and your spiritual strength, this union cannot accomplish all it is capable of.

In a particular section of the Talmud, called *Masechet Yevamot* 63a, Rabbi Yossi meets Elijah the Prophet and asks him what the words, "a helpmate corresponding to him," mean. Elijah responds that the woman brings light to the man's eyes and helps him stand on his feet. Without the woman, the man cannot accomplish the purpose for which he came into this world. Look how important you are! When each individual within this bond lives up to their purpose, the Torah says, *"V'hayoo lebasar echad"* ("והיו לבשר אחד.")— "And they shall become one flesh" (Genesis 2:24). You will feel as though you are one, working together to accomplish your collective goals. You will have a unified purpose, recognize each other's strengths as well as weaknesses, and do all this through love, commitment, and honesty.

There is an ancient custom practiced in the land of Israel that when a girl is born, a pine or a cypress tree is planted in her honor, and when a boy is born, a cedar tree is planted. When they find each other and are married, the branches from these trees are used as their wedding canopy. Could it possibly be that God is the ultimate matchmaker?

Congratulations—*Mazel tov*!

Your Personal Lev Moment

1. Make a list of the ways your groom would appreciate your help.
2. Looking at the list you created, what do you already do? Do you think you could do more?

3. How do you think you can become "one flesh"? It may take you years to feel that unity, as it builds up slowly—sharing "*oys*" and joys together. Every day you grow closer. Some days you may feel you are getting farther from this goal. Do not be discouraged and think it is not possible. Try to think of what you represent—spiritual strength—and stick to it. Bring the light to the marriage and to each other.

Author's daughter, Hadas, escorted by her parents

"לֵב חָכָם יַשְׂכִּיל פִּיהוּ וְעַל־שְׂפָתָיו יוֹסִיף לֶקַח."
"The heart of a wise man gives his mouth
intelligence and adds learning to his lips."
(Proverbs 16:23)

Mom Speaks
Bar/Bat Mitzvah

I n every *Brit Milah* (circumcision ceremony) Jews say, "This little
one will be mighty." In Hebrew, it is *"Zeh hakatan gadol yeheye"*
("זה הקטן גדול יהיה") (*The Complete Artscroll Siddur*, p. 212).

Why do we say this? The obvious answer is the size. A newborn is
tiny. But there is a much more meaningful reason hidden here. Little
ones—as much as they give us immense joy, unconditional love, and
laughter—are concerned only with their own needs: who is going to
feed them, pick them up, or change their diapers. When we are young,
our circle of influence and control is limited. We give happiness to
those near us, those who naturally love us. However, "big" people—
people who live independently and who contribute to the society in
which they live—are concerned with other matters. They are the ones
who have the ability and the means to help others. They are the leaders

who make this world a better place because of their presence—that is their greatness.

The words *big (gadol)* and *greatness (gedula)* in Hebrew share the same root: *gimmel, dalet,* and *lamed* (ג.ד.ל). Understanding that Hebrew words that share the same roots are indeed connected sheds light on this magnificent connection. Being "big" can lead to greatness. Greatness can occur as we develop our skills of living and thriving in this world.

Speaking of hidden meaning behind words, I would be remiss if I do not share one more Hebrew gem. The word for "coincidence" in Hebrew is *mikreh* (מקרה). When you divide this word, the *mi* (מ) means "from." The last letter, the *hey* (ה), represents God in this world. And the middle of the word, the *kre (קרה)*, means "happened." So what does the complete word *mikreh* mean? This word translates as "happened from God." To me, this means that there are no coincidences in this world of ours. We are put here for a purpose, one which only we can fulfill.

With what shall I bless you? What shall I wish for you on this very special day in your life? The name of your Bar Mitzvah *Shabbat* is *Naso.* This particular word is the answer. *Naso* is a verb; it commands a person to lift up their head and be counted among the Israelites. I wish for you to continue to lift up your head and be proud of who you are and what you stand for. I wish for you *anavah v'ga'avah* (ענווה וגאווה), humility and pride. Be proud of where you came from and be humble to reach the places you want to go!

Mazel tov!

The author's youngest son, Yaniv, on his Bar Mitzvah weekend

Your Personal Lev Moment

1. Think of an occasion when you provided *nachat* (emotional pleasure) to someone else: What was the behavior? Who was the fortunate beneficiary?

2. Name a recent time when you felt you were a "big" person: What was the action you had to take? Would you do it again?

3. Think about the people you love. Can you discern a behavior that others do to show their greatness? Do you acknowledge them for this?

 "In Jewish history there are no coincidences."
–Elie Wiesel

You CAN Create Light
Final Words

As I reflect on all that has happened from the time I began this project to today, I am amazed at life's twists and turns. This journey began with my sister Bruria and her diagnosis of cancer. Her diagnosis was followed by the same diagnosis in my mom, a year later. My oldest sister, Ronit, was then diagnosed with breast cancer one week following my mom. It was a trial time for my family, that is for sure. All three are now healed, thank God!

I left my work of the past sixteen years as an Education Director to pursue new avenues and spread the love of Judaism to more people, both Jews and non-Jews. I believe that Judaism has wisdom to share with all of humanity—each and every one of us is a product of the intricate tapestry of what we call "life."

The Book of Genesis holds the story of our collective beginning.

"בְּרֵאשִׁית בָּרָא אֱלֹהִים אֵת הַשָּׁמַיִם וְאֵת הָאָרֶץ: וְהָאָרֶץ הָיְתָה תֹהוּ וָבֹהוּ וְחֹשֶׁךְ
עַל־פְּנֵי תְהוֹם וְרוּחַ אֱלֹהִים מְרַחֶפֶת עַל־פְּנֵי הַמָּיִם."

*"Beresheet bara Elohim et Hashamyim v'et Haaretz; V'ha'aretz ha'yita
tohoo v'vohoo, v'choshech al p'nai tehom v'ruach Elohim merachefet al p'nai
hamayim."*

"In the beginning of God's creating the Heavens and the Earth—
when the Earth was astonishingly empty, with darkness upon the
surface of the deep, and the Divine Presence hovered upon the surface
of the waters—God said, 'Let there be light,' and there was light"
(Genesis 1:1–2).

When God began the act of creation, darkness was the state of
the universe. The word *bara*, or "formed," teaches us that God forms
something out of nothing.

Let's contrast this with another verse in the Bible, a verse that the
rabbis thought was important to add to our daily morning prayers. In
Isaiah 45:7, it is said:

"יוֹצֵר אוֹר וּבוֹרֵא חֹשֶׁךְ."

"Yotzer or oovoreh choshech."

"Who forms light and creates darkness."

Isaiah uses two words to convey the word *create*: *yotzer*, which
technically translates as "form," and *boreh,* which translates as "create."
Why use these two words? Why doesn't it say that God simply created
darkness and light? In other words, why can't we say *boreh* for both?
After all, God formed darkness and light.

There is an unparalleled wisdom to the Hebrew language.
Ramban, also known as Nachmanides, was a Spanish Talmudist,
Kabbalist, and biblical commentator during the thirteenth century.
Through his commentary on the Book of Genesis, we discover the
difference between these two seemingly similar words. The word *boreh*
is the ability to create something from nothing, an ability only God
possesses. Only God can form darkness. *Yotzer,* on the other hand, is

to take something that exists and create a new product in order to give it its purpose. That gift is bestowed on us by God. We humans can do this. We can take a substance, such as wheat, and create bread. We can take energy and create electricity. While *boreh* is an attribute of God, *yotzer* is a godly-given attribute that humans possess and therefore can emulate God. And what did God *yotzer*? Light! And because He has created light, we as humans can bring this Divine light into our lives—by our thoughts, by our actions, and by our demeanor!

I am comforted by the concept that darkness is something none of us can create. Only God can form darkness. Darkness is simply a state where there is no light. It gives me immense hope to realize that we humans can bring light, in the metaphorical sense. Perhaps as you read these words, you feel you are surrounded by darkness or that your future might not seem bright and hopeful. Don't be discouraged, dear reader! You have the ability to bring light into a situation and help illuminate our world.

In the Talmud, it is written:

”נר לאחד נר למאה.“

"Ner l'echad, ner l'me'ah."

"Candle for one, candle for many" (*Masechet Shabbat* 122a).

One small candle can light the way for a hundred people.

My blessing and wish for each of you is that your life is a "candle," bringing light to all around you!

With all my *lev*,

Dorice Horenstein

A Note from my Sister

Part 2

Three years ago, I won… Yes, I won! I won a journey few people go through in this stage of their lives. I was merited to know who will always be by my side and from whom I need to depart. I met incredible women, some of whom are not physically with me today, but they had significant and memorable parts in my own victory. I learned that my body, which, at first, I was very upset with, did not desert me, but fought together with me! And for that I am eternally grateful.

And most importantly… to my family, who throughout this time (and it was not a short time), was the wind behind me pushing me forward. They lifted me up every time I fell, cheered me, and supported me. So, to you, THANK YOU!

So, dear girlfriends and loving family, make sure you get a yearly check-up and listen to your body. It speaks to you!

My sister Bruria on a vacation
in Paris in 2018, cancer free!

This is my sister Bruria's
note on Facebook 2017.

About the Author

Dorice Horenstein is a master teacher. She arrived in Portland, Oregon, from Israel, after meeting her soon-to-be husband while volunteering in a kibbutz.

In the States, she received her BA in English Literature and a certificate in Teaching English as a second language. She taught hundreds of children and adults, Jews and non-Jews, the gems of Judaism, with an emphasis on the Hebrew language.

Dorice has worked in synagogues and a private school, led sessions for NewCAJE and Spring Conference of the North by Northwest Region of Women's League of Conservative Judaism organizations, and was the Education Director at a synagogue in Portland, Oregon, for sixteen years.

Together with her husband, they have three children. She enjoys dancing in her spare time.

References

Throughout this book, there are citations from four main sources: the Torah (תורה, the first five books of the Bible), the Bible, or as it is called in Hebrew, *Tanach* (תנ"ך, often referred to as the "Old Testament" by non-Jews), the *Siddur* (סידור, the Jewish prayer book Jews use to pray daily, on the Sabbath, and during holidays), and the Babylonian Talmud (תלמוד בבלי, the primary source of Jewish rabbinic law, consisting of the *Mishnah* and the *Gemara,* which were compiled in approximately 500 AD, or "CE," typically when spoken by Jews). I have also used several citations from *Ethics of the Fathers,* known in Hebrew as *Pirkei Avot,* a compilation of ethical teachings from the Talmud. I use these two titles interchangeably throughout my book.

For the Torah, I referenced *The Artscroll Stone Edition,* translated by Rabbi Nosson Scherman and Rabbi Meir Zlotowitz and published by Mesorah Publications (Brooklyn, New York: 1998). For the Bible, I referenced the English translation of the entire *Tanach* (תנ"ך). *The*

Complete Tanakh was translated by Rabbi A.J. Rosenberg and can be found on www.chabad.org. For the *Siddur*, I chose *The Complete Artscroll Siddur*, translated by Rabbi Nosson Scherman and published by Mesorah Publications (Brooklyn, New York: 1986). When quoting the Talmud, I relied on *The William Davidson Talmud* that can be found on www.sefaria.org. Using this online resource allowed me to easily access various Talmudic sources for my writing. On a few occasions, I chose to translate words myself when I needed to point out something within the Hebrew language. As *Pirkei Avot* is inserted into many prayer books, I used *The Complete Artscroll Siddur* to translate all of the *Pirkei Avot* sources.

My Personal Lev Moment

1. Rabbi Noah Weinberg was the Orthodox Jewish dean and founder of *Aish HaTorah* website, www.aish.com.

Chamber One

1. *Midrash Tanchuma, Vayakhel* 1.
2. Dena Weinberg is the wife (*Rebbetzin*) of *Aish HaTorah's* founder Rabbi Noah Weinberg. She is the founder and dean of EYAHT College of Jewish Studies for Women in Jerusalem.
3. Joel Lurie Grishaver, *Stories We Pray* (Los Angeles: Torah Aura Production, 2012), 28. (Taken from *Midrash Ha'Gadol* 1, 74.)
4. Rabbi Joseph Telushkin, *Jewish Wisdom* (New York City: William Morrow and Company, Inc., 1994), 200.
5. Anne Frank, *The Diary of a Young Girl* (New York City: Pocket Books/Simon & Schuster, Inc., 1953), 234.

Chamber Two

1. Rabbi Joseph Telushkin, *Rebbe: The Life and Teaching of Menachem M. Schneerson, The Most Influential Rabbi in Modern History* (New York City: Harper Wave, 2014), 251.
2. Israel Meir Kagan (also known as the Hafetz Hayim, or Chofetz Chaim), *Mishnah Berurah, Siman* 581:1.
3. Rabbi Hanoch Teller, *The Courtrooms of the Mind: Stories and Advice on Judging Others Favorably* (New York City Publishing Company, 1991), xix.
4. Rabbi Attar, also known as Rabbi Hayyim ben Moshe ibn Attar, composed the *Or HaChaim,* a commentary on the first five books of the Bible. This specific reference is based on his commentary of Exodus 2:2. Rabbi Attar was born in the seventeenth century and was of Moroccan descent. His work is translated by Eliyahu Munk. You can find more information on www.sefaria.org.

Chamber Three

1. Gary Chapman, *The 5 Love Languages* (Chicago: Northfield Publishing, 1992).
2. Ahad Ha'am, *Siddur* (Young Judaea, 1993), 152. Ahad Ha'am was a poet and Zionist.
3. Rabbi Sidney Greenberg, *The Wisdom of Modern Rabbis* (New York City: Kensington Publishing Corp., 2001), 9. Rabbi Greenberg quoted Rabbi Hertz within his book. Rabbi Hertz was the chief rabbi of England from 1913 until his death in 1946.

Hebrew—The Language of Intent
Power and Secret of the Hebrew Letters

First time it appears in the Torah	Meaning	Numerical Value	Sound	Look / Shape	Letter Name
Eloyim, God	Champion	1	Silent	א	Alef
Bara, Created	House	2	B	ב	Bet
Gadol, Big	Camel	3	G (as in God)	ג	Gimmel
Deshe, Grass	Door	4	D	ד	Dalet
He-lachem lechem, Here you have food	Give	5	H	ה	Hey
Vavei hamishkan, The hooks of the Tabernacle	Hook	6	V	ו	Vav
Zera, Seed	Sward	7	Z	ז	Zayin

First time it appears in the Torah	Meaning	Numerical Value	Sound	Look / Shape	Letter Name
Choshech, Darkness	Unified	8	Ch	ח	Chet
Yom, Day	Hand	10	Y	י	Yud
Kutnot, Skin garments	Palm of Hand	20	K	כ	Kaf
Layla, Night	Study	30	L	ל	Lamed
Mayim, Water	Water	40	M	מ	Mem
Nefresh, Soul	Faithful	50	N	נ	Nun
Sovev, Surround	Support Protection	60	S	ס	Samech
Erev, Evening	Seeing	70	Silent	ע	Ayin

First time it appears in the Torah	Meaning	Numerical Value	Sound	Look / Shape	Letter Name
Pnai Tehom, The surface of the deep	Mouth, Speak	80	P	פ	Peh
Tziviticha, Commanded you	Righteous	90	TZ	צ	Tzadik
Kedem, Ancient	Holy	100	K	ק	Kuf
Ruach, Wind	Head	200	R	ר	Resh
Shamayim, Heavens, Sky	Tooth	300	Sh	ש	Shin
Tohu, Astonishingly empty	Truth	400	T	ת	Tav
			Ch/K	ך	Final Chaf
			M	ם	Final Mem

First time it appears in the Torah	Meaning	Numerical Value	Sound	Look / Shape	Letter Name
			N	ן	Final Nun
			F	ף	Final Fey
			TZ	ץ	Final Tzadik

CPSIA information can be obtained
at www.ICGtesting.com
Printed in the USA
BVHW070224160219
540441BV00001B/2/P